ARCHITECTURE ASIA

Journal of the Architects Regional Council Asia (ARCASIA)

Contents

Editorial

In 2023, *Architecture Asia* updated its publication plan with a series of topically tied "national (or regional) issue + forum," publication models in order to further increase the visibility of the member institutes of the Architects Regional Council Asia (ARCASIA). This new plan, with its focus on contemporary architectural development in specific Asian regions, intends to gradually shape the discourse structure of contemporary Asian architecture "from one to many levels" to make its research and "mapping" possible. Thanks to the suggestions of The Association of Siamese Architects under Royal Patronage (ASA), the first issue of this new publication plan takes shape as an issue and forum on contemporary architecture in Thailand. This new publication plan also marks the beginning of thematic discussions on contemporary architectural development among Asian countries and regions.

We extend thanks to the support of ASA and its nominees, Jenchieh Hung, and his partner Kulthida Songkittipakdee, who are both also close friends of *Architecture Asia*. Nominated as guest editors to organize this first issue and forum themed "Thailand Contemporary Architecture," Hung and Songkittipakdee, as local practicing architects, introduce the emergence and development of Thai architecture, and share for publication and discussion, a significant group of architects and their architectural projects that represent Thai architectural diversity.

The concept of "Thai-ness" has been proposed to define the characteristics of contemporary Thai architecture. It is clear that this term is dynamic and polysemous. On the one hand, it stands for uniqueness in the Asian context since it carries "free, dynamic, and futuristic" connotations; on the other hand, it is identifiable in the global context as it shows strong regional cultural features and a sense of natural ambiance.

This issue explores the ideological roots of equal emphasis on the "traditional" and "avant-garde" features of contemporary Thai architecture, which was directly influenced by Western modernism in the early stage, and which later went through the gradual evolution of regional philosophies. It's fair to say that the reforms of Thai architecture and design directly reflect social phenomena, such as the formation of national consciousness, the development of economic industries, and the uprising of new media. Thai architecture exhibits a high degree of unity in form, space, construction, and expression by fusing modernism, regionalism, and futurism.

Meanwhile, Thai architecture also presents the conflict and harmony between the "natural environment" and the "human-made environment." Thai architects' participation in natural construction and transmission of natural information as their reverence to and exploration of nature echo Thailand's unique climate and culture. Besides, the complex urban and rural landscapes of Thailand inspire architects to reshape the relationship between human and nature, to recollect tranquility of mind in highly dense urban areas, and to explore the humbleness of human beings in the natural rural environment.

Profiles

HAS design and research was founded by **Jenchieh Hung** and **Kulthida Songkittipakdee**, and they explore Asia's architectural language through a parallel "design + research" approach. The practice emphasizes the analogy of nature and artificially created nature, looking for another kind of new natural architecture through the city's own derivatives, which HAS has named "The Improvised, MANufAcTURE, and Chameleon Architecture."

The work of **Hung And Songkittipakdee (HAS)** encompasses cultural buildings, religious architecture, installation art, exhibition design, and experimental projects. HAS's research includes the train and railway markets, charming roadside vendors, the borderless illegal constructions under elevated freeways, and the roundabouts of dead alleys. These interesting scenes, typically existing in Asian cities, reveal how through temporary constructions people find a "new" norm in a reinforced-concrete city.

HAS has developed an international reputation by winning competitions; their work stands by synthesizing form, pattern, material, and technology into irreducible constructions. They have been widely recognized for their innovative work and have received awards and honors such as the Thailand Prestige Award 2021, DOTY Award 2019, Design Star Award 2018, Distinguished Alumni Award 2016, as well as their inclusion into *Wallpaper* Architects' Directory* 2022.

Hung and Songkittipakdee have also been actively involved in academia as visiting professors and architecture design critics for Tongji University, China, as well as Chulalongkorn University, Thailand, and King Mongkut's University of Technology in Thonburi, Thailand. They were also invited to serve as curators and critics for Thai contemporary architecture, executing a series of exhibitions, publications, and forums, and were commended by the Ministry of Foreign Affairs Thailand as Chinese-Thai architecture influencers.

Guest editors:
Jenchieh Hung (left) and
Kulthida Songkittipakdee (right)

Chatpong "Chat" Chuenrudeemol obtained his Bachelor of Arts in Architecture from University of California, Berkeley, United States, in 1994 and his Master of Architecture from Harvard Graduate School of Design, United States, in 2000. After completing his studies in the US, Chuenrudeemol returned to his birthplace, Bangkok, Thailand, to form **CHAT Architects**, a practice that combines research and design, resulting in innovative multiscalar projects that aim to stimulate community through strategies that reinterpret authentic local conditions. In 2015, he created CHAT lab, a research think tank aimed at discovering new Thai vernacular "street" typologies, affectionately titling the first project "Bangkok Bastards."

In 2020, Chuenrudeemol received Thailand's Silpathorn Award, the country's highest award for contemporary artists presented by the Ministry of Culture of Thailand. He was also awarded an ASA gold medal as "Thailand's Emerging Architect" in

2017, presented by The Association of Siamese Architects under Royal Patronage (ASA). In 2020, CHAT Architect's Samsen STREET Hotel project won the Building of the Year Award (Asia Pacific region) in the INDE.Awards. Chuenrudeemol's work has been exhibited both at home and abroad, including in Japan's TOTO Gallery Ma in 2015, in the gallery's 30th Anniversary exhibition themed "The Asian Everyday."

Chuenrudeemol has taught at the design schools of various universities throughout the world, including INDA (International Program in Design and Architecture) at Chulalongkorn University, Thailand, National University of Singapore (NUS), Singapore, and Massachusetts Institute of Technology (MIT), United States. Currently, he serves as an adjunct associate professor at Taylor's University, Kuala Lumpur, Malaysia, guiding students in the research of "Kuala Lumpur Bastards."

Chomchon Fusinpaiboon is an assistant professor at the Faculty of Architecture, Chulalongkorn University, Thailand, and a practicing architect. He received his Bachelor in Architecture from Chulalongkorn University. After completing his master's in architecture in urban design at the Bartlett School of Architecture, University College London, United Kingdom, he worked briefly at Atelier of Architects in Bangkok, Thailand. In 2014, he attained a PhD from Sheffield University, United Kingdom, with a dissertation that examined how a modern architectural culture has been established in Thailand, and how it has transformed traditional ideas of architecture and vice versa.

His current research interests cover Asian modern and contemporary architecture—especially lesser-known, overlooked, and understated ones, despite their possible contributions to the history, theory, and the practice of architecture in Asia. He has also published a book and a book chapter on the unconventional works and ideas of Thai architect Prince Vodhyakara Varavarn, who

reinterpreted the English Arts and Crafts philosophy to adapt it for modern Thai architecture from both prewar and postwar periods. His published academic papers include research on the establishment of Thailand's first architecture school that involved nationalism, a Belgian architect, and Chinese migrants, and research on the history and renovation of the shophouse, a non-pedigree modern architecture that played a major role in the urbanization of Thailand during the 1960s and 1970s, questioning its legacy and its future in relation to contemporary architectural practice and urban issues.

Teaming up with partner **Hyunju Jang** as **DRFJ (Design & Research by Fusinpaiboon & Jang)**, Fusinpaiboon has continued design research on shophouse renovation in Bangkok with minimal involvement of an architect, aiming at scaling up decent yet affordable shophouse renovation. The practice exhibited the work as Shophouse2Go! at the 2022 Hong Kong Shenzhen Bi-City Biennale of Urbanism \ Architecture (Hong Kong), which was themed "Seeds of Resilience – Re(dis)covering the City."

Philip Cornwel-Smith, a British writer based in Bangkok, Thailand, received his Bachelor of Arts (Honors) in History from Sheffield University, United Kingdom, in 1986. While a student, he completed the UK's first course offered in world history, worked for the award-winning student magazine *Arrows*, and wrote his dissertation on "Modern Movement design in the 1920s." His publishing career in London, United Kingdom included editing works on heritage and history, as well as biographies. At Time Out Publications in 1989–91, Cornwel-Smith was assistant, then deputy editor of the Time Out city guides to London and Amsterdam, The Netherlands, writing about their landmark buildings. When Cornwel-Smith was appointed founding editor in 1994 of *Bangkok Metro*, the Thai capital's first city listings magazine, he covered many issues of urbanism and heritage.

Since becoming a freelancer in 2002, he has continued residing in Bangkok. Cornwel-Smith has written about architecture in many publications; also as the editor of *Thailand Travellers' Companion*, columnist in *Bangkok 101*, and as contributor to the *Dorling Kindersley Guide to Thailand*. He has also analyzed the design of the US embassy in Thailand for *World Architecture* magazine. More recently, he has covered the built environment in his books *Very Thai: Everyday Popular Culture* and *Very Bangkok: In the City of the Senses*. As a recognized expert in Thai culture, he has guest-lectured at numerous universities, including Chulalongkorn and Thammasat Universities in Thailand, and the School of Oriental and African Studies (SOAS) in London, and has been interviewed in several international documentaries, often talking about urban issues.

Plan Architect was founded in 1975 by a group of architects that was bound together by a passion to create innovative and socially responsible architectural designs. We believe that a commitment to excellence could be combined with a commitment to Thai society. In a constantly and rapidly changing world, research never ends; neither does the challenge of applying new ideas to new technology, so Plan Architect is always on the cutting edge of innovative design.

The constant flow and exchange of ideas and knowledge of our team shapes our practice's spirit. We are not only open to fresh perspectives, different techniques, and the wisdom of experience; we also actively seek it out in each member of our team. Over our forty years in practice, Plan Architect has grown from a small studio to become a well-established business.

However, we do not let success limit us by thinking that we have reached our full potential. There is still a long way yet to go and we will continue reaching for the sky with our feet planted firmly on the ground. We are constantly learning from the projects we design, the business partners we work with, and our colleagues. We respect each other's input and relish new challenges.

We believe in an organization that is founded on friendship and mutual respect. Each member of our whole is encouraged to develop along his or her own potential.

Our team members are motivated to produce their best work and this forms the foundation and cornerstone of our practice, through which we create life-affirming designs that benefit our clients, users, and us (by way of rewarding us with immense job satisfaction). A design is a success only when it satisfies the client, the design team, and its community. All parties are given importance during the creative process, because a lone architect cannot design in a vacuum.

Every person at Plan Architect shares a commitment to social responsibility. We make our contributions through our designs, social activities, and by initiating and supporting educational and cultural programs.

The new Plan generation is offered plenty of scope to test its ideas and initiative; responsibility and growth are always encouraged. Like all families, our children are our future.

Architects 49 Limited (A49) was established in 1983 by **Nithi Sthapitanonda**, whose vision is to create timeless architecture with clean simplicity. Based in Bangkok, Thailand, we currently have over 200 staff and studios established in other parts of Thailand—Phuket and Chiang Mai (2004) and Khon Kaen (2015). Our diverse team enables us to take on a variety of projects in areas that range from residential, commercial, retail, education, hospitality, and health. Our portfolio also includes several large-scale mixed-use projects, both in Asia and the Middle East. To keep abreast of the times and maintain our position as a leading architecture firm, we are focused on sustainable, human-centric designs—each with its respective distinctive character—using the latest architectural and technical advances. We strive to embark on a journey of data-driven design by utilizing technologies. One of the schemes that we have implemented is the use of artificial intelligence (AI) and machine learning in our workflow, while empowering our employees with the required knowledge and motivation to achieve our goals.

President and Managing Director **Prabhakorn Vadanyakul** attained his Bachelor of Architecture from Chulalongkorn University, Thailand. Following further studies at Catholic University of America in Washington, United States, he graduated with a Master of Architecture. He has since been responsible for a wide range of projects, with his work extending to the United Arab Emirates and India, increasing breadth of A49's project portfolio.

Main project architect and Deputy Managing Director **Somkiat Lochindapong** brings with him an extensive experience in designing, which he has applied to many major projects in Thailand and overseas. He received his bachelor's degree from Silpakorn University, Thailand, and earned his master's degree from the University of California, Los Angeles, United States. After seven years of independent work, he joined A49 as a senior architect in 2005 and was later promoted to director at Architects 49 International in 2007.

Duangrit Bunnag Architect Limited (DBALP) was established on July 2, 1998, as an innovative and small design firm. The practice has evolved over many years to today present itself as structured tactical design "groups" that make up the Architect Group, Interior Design Group, Landscape Architect Group, and Technician Group. These groups work cohesively on a "project team" basis assigned to projects. All the design principles of each project is supervised by Design Director **Duangrit Bunnag**.

DBALP's works follow these design principles:

Simplicity—Simplicity is not simple. Only those who pursue simplicity may find their project simplistic. Architecture with simplicity may be a result of a very complex form.

Function—All practical architecture develop around good functional plans. It is in the practice's interest to develop a proper functional plan in each project, to allow the project's best space utilization.

Good idea—Every project needs at least one good idea. Without an idea, one cannot define architecture from buildings.

The new—There must be something new in each project that enforces its difference from other projects. If you are going to create a project, you are therewith obligated to create something new.

Walllasia is an architectural studio based in Bangkok, Thailand. With over twenty years of experience, we are determined to integrate architecture and landscape design deeply into society, in terms of culture, economics, the environment, and nature.

We believe that ready access to architecture is essential for everyone, and that every detail in the process—from planning and design to the finished project—constitutes an artform that entails a relationship and a dialogue between design and construction. It is an art in which new techniques are created, and every possible obstacle is overcome.

At Walllasia, we combine our strengths in construction technique, art, intuition, and the applied philosophy of nature to create balanced works that exist comfortably between the business and the art.

We also specialize in landscape design, especially in matching architecture to the environment. We know precisely how to select the most appropriate green element, like mature trees, or the best natural materials, such as stones, and the most evoking constructed components, such as sculptures and building materials, so that all complement each other's best attributes.

We create spaces that are tailor-made to meet the client's needs in harmony with nature.

Boonserm Premthada, founder of **Bangkok Project Studio**, is an architect and artist and also an adjunct assistant professor at Columbia University Graduate School of Architecture, Planning and Preservation (GSAPP), New York, United States, and the Department of Architecture, The University of Hong Kong, Hong Kong SAR, China.

Premthada's work has won many international awards and accolades, which include Winner, 2011 ar+d Awards for Emerging Architecture, presented by the *Architectural Review*, London, United Kingdom; Shortlisted, Aga Khan Award for Architecture 2013, Geneva, Switzerland; Grand prize and "Special Solution" category winner, International Brick Architecture 2014, Wiesenberger, Vienna, Austria; Overall winner and "Hospitality" category winner, The Plan Award 2017, Italy; Winner, Global Award for Sustainable Architecture 2018, under the Patronage of UNESCO and Cité de l'architecture et du patrimoine, Paris, France; Winner, The Royal Academy Dorfman Awards 2019, The Royal Academy of Arts, London, United Kingdom; Winner: "Best Sanctuary," for Elephant World, 2021 Wallpaper* Design Awards, London, United Kingdom; Golden Madonnina, "Social Impact" category, THE DESIGN PRIZE 2021, Milan, Italy; and "Best Restaurant" winner, 2022 Wallpaper* Design Awards for The Artisans Ayutthaya: The Women Restaurant.

Premthada has lectured and exhibited at the Royal Institute of British Architects (RIBA) (United Kingdom), Cité de l'architecture et du patrimoine (Paris, France), the Hongkong Pavilion as part of the 16th International Architecture Exhibition in Venice, Italy, École Polytechnique Fédérale de Lausanne (EPFL) (Switzerland), University of Tokyo (Japan), University of Hong Kong (Hong Kong SAR, China), National University of Singapore (Singapore), the Bartlett School of Architecture, University College London (United Kingdom), Columbia University (United States), and several other international institutions. His pavilion for the project The House for Human and The House for Elephants represented Thailand at Biennale Architettura 2021. In 2022, his Elephant Theatre was exhibited at the Biennale of Architecture and Landscape Design, Versailles, France. His Elephant Dung Brick installation was also a part of the 254th Summer Exhibition of the Royal Academy of Arts, United Kingdom.

Department of ARCHITECTURE Co. is a design studio based in Bangkok, Thailand. Founded by **Amata Luphaiboon** and **Twitee Vajrabhaya Teparkum** in 2004, Department of Architecture Co. practices architecture, interior architecture, landscape architecture, and other related design disciplines in a broad range of programmatic requirements and scales.

The studio's design approach encompasses not only the tangible aspects of architecture, but also the conceptual framework upon which individuals interact. The practice is interested in finding new possibilities for architecture by exploring beyond the surface to design underlying foundations that form the basis for physical spaces.

IDIN Architects (IDIN) was founded in 2004. Our name forms the acronym for "Integrating Design Into Nature." We perceive nature in two ways: it can be defined as the ecology around us and it can also refer to the innate mannerisms and personalities of people. IDIN's design philosophy directs its attention toward merging this sense of surroundings and innate characteristics with architectural aesthetic. This union is achieved through a process of analyzing and prioritizing the different needs and requirements of each project.

In Thai, "I-DIN" refers to the beautiful scent that emanates after rainfall, perfectly implying the tropical climate of Thailand. Within this context, our name IDIN references Thailand's tropical climate, which is an aspect IDIN's designs aim to respond to. Our emphasis is, therefore, placed not only on aesthetics, but also on being practical, so as to suit our tropical environment.

IDIN Architects' founding principal, **Jeravej Hongsakul** received a Bachelor of Architecture in 1998 from King Mongkut's Institute of Technology, Lat Krabang, Thailand, and has been practicing since 2000. IDIN became well-known in the Thai architecture scene for the project Phuket Gateway, which received an Architectural Design Award in 2010 from The Association of Siamese Architects under Royal Patronage (ASA). Since then, many projects from our company have continually been honored with numerous prizes, both at national and international levels: ASA Architectural Design Awards in 2016 and 2020, The Plan Award in 2020 and 2021, Architizer A+ Awards in 2016, 2017, 2019, 2020, and 2021, American Architecture Prize in 2017, ARCASIA Awards for Architecture in 2016, 2018, 2020, and 2021, 2A Asia Architecture Award in 2017, Design for Asia Awards 2020 and 2021, German Design Award in 2018, GOOD Design Award 2021, and The Prix Versailles South Asia and the Pacific 2020 by UNESCO and the International Union of Architects.

Vin Varavarn Architects (VVA) is a Bangkok-based architectural practice established in Thailand in 2005 by **M. L. Varudh Varavarn**. VVA is involved in a variety of design projects that range from categories like residential, commercial, and social responsibility. The practice's work is recognized for simplicity of architecture, the value of local materials, and the appropriation of craftsmanship, along with the emphasis on context and the imaginative use of materials. Many of their work have been widely published and have received many international awards.

In 2017, the Post Disaster School project was selected as the winner of the 8th International Biennial Barbara Cappochin Prize of Architecture. In 2018, the project was nominated for the RIBA International List by The Royal Institute of British Architects. In 2021, the PANNAR Sufficiency Economic and Agriculture Learning Center project was selected as Best Design Award winner in The Golden Pin Design Award; it also received an ASA gold medal for "Sustainable Architecture" by The Association of Siamese Architects under Royal Patronage (ASA) in 2022.

Varavarn believes in always being involved in social and community improvement and aligns his ideas with the work of his practice. He enthusiastically involves himself in CSR work with different non-profit organizations and foundations to design schools and low-cost housing for local communities in different remote areas all over Thailand. In 2018, Varavarn was appointed chief curator for the Thai Pavilion at the 16th Venice Architecture Biennale. This year, he was awarded the Silpathorn Award in the field of architecture, an honor presented to Thai contemporary artists by the Office of Contemporary Art and Culture, Ministry of Culture of Thailand.

all(zone), based in Bangkok Thailand, is a group of design professionals made up of people who are fascinated by the ever-changing mega metropolises that give form to their everyday life. Their observations are always captured by contemporary vernacular design solutions, leading them to create built environments where all can feel "at home" in the world.

Their international participations include exhibitions at Guggenheim Museum in New York (United States), Chicago Architecture Biennial (United States), Vitra Design Museum (Germany), Art Institute of Chicago (United States), the Triennale di Milano (Italy), Echigo-Tsumori Art Triennale (Japan), Sharjah Architecture Triennial (United Arab Emirates), and La Casa Encendida in Madrid (Spain).

In 2016, all(zone) completed MAIIAM Contemporary Art Museum, the first contemporary art museum in Thailand. The practice has been included in the 2019 100+ Best Architecture Firms list compiled by *Domus* and was awarded the Top 50 Best Design 2021 Award by *Monocle* magazine for a project in Bangkok. They were also commissioned to design the 2022 MPavilion in Melbourne, Australia.

Stu/D/O Architects (Stu/D/O), based in Bangkok, Thailand, is an architectural design studio whose practice traverses the fields of architecture, urbanism, and sustainable design. Grounded in the belief that architecture should consider all the layers of physical and cultural distinctness in each site, the office does not adopt a fixed design process, but instead focuses on a strong studio culture that pools together fresh ideas to result in new design approaches and new possibilities of creating space. Founded under the desire to create architecture that sustains itself, and the community along with it, Stu/D/O's work reflects the importance of the human experience within the creation, as well as the complexities of the constructed environment.

Having graduated from the Architectural Association School of Architecture (AA) in the United Kingdom—specializing in sustainable design— and Massachusetts Institute of Technology—majoring in architecture and urbanism, co-founders **Chanasit Cholasuek** (the "D" quotient) and **Apichart Srirojanapinyo** (the "O" quotient) established Stu/D/O Architects in 2010 with the belief that a collaborative working environment leads to unrestrictive design thinking that allows for the freedom to explore new possibilities of architecture. With its team of passionate architects, designers and engineers, Stu/D/O has designed, and is currently involved in, both local and international projects across an array of design typologies. These include a wide range of design projects, from small exhibition designs to private residences to large commercial buildings.

Since its establishment, Stu/D/O has received various awards and international recognition for their architectural work, which include the World Architecture Festival (WAF) Award for two consecutive years: in 2018, for InterCrop Headquarter, in the "Office Building" category and in 2017, for Naiipa Art Complex, in the "Mixed Used" category. Naiipa Art Complex was also selected as an Honorable Mention entry in the 2017 ARCASIA Awards for Architecture, for a Citation Award in 2016 from The Association of Siamese Architects under Royal Patronage (ASA), and won Building of the Year in 2015 in the Wallpaper* Design Awards.

Patchara + Ornnicha Architecture (POAR) is a Nonthaburi (Thailand)-based multidisciplinary architecture studio founded by **Patchara Wongboonsin** and **Ornnicha Duriyaprapan** in 2012. POAR expresses the dialogues around architecture, centered on a core of how architecture can impact and strengthen the identity of urbanity, the local community, and a regional scale.

POAR seeks to define and identify the forgotten spirit of place by reflecting the intricate cultural backdrop of Thailand, while crafting a new expression that fulfills the identity of the community.

EKAR Architects believes that architecture originates from the perfect mixture of beautiful aesthetic sense and functional usability, through a thinking process, analysis, and connections based on different conditions and contexts that surround every dimension of each specific location. Our physical identities remain in the shade of life. We see the preciousness of life. Our creativity is influenced by the contexts that shape and give life. We craft lives and gently place the design on the specific context, using detailed research as a documentary of these lives, embracing them in an ongoing vision. The designs are driven by not just their present, but also their past and future. The designs created by the practice are constantly operating and influencing, wandering alongside people's journeys. We believe that as time passes, the value of the design becomes more apparent.

EKAR Architects' recent projects, spanning categories like renovation, mixed-use and commercial buildings, and private residences focus on user experiences and their requirements, and are especially steered toward a simple lifestyle and a clean form and space design. Over the last few years, the practice has become a breakthrough architectural firm with many successful projects and accolades under its belt, which includes winning the 40 under 40 Awards in 2018.

Other awards that gained the practice worldwide recognition include the Ar House Award in 2022 and 2021, World Architecture Festival (WAF) Award in 2022 and 2017, Dezeen Award in 2022, The International Architecture Award in 2022, presented by The Chicago Athenaeum: Museum of Architecture and Design in the United States (together with The European Center for Architecture Art Design and Urban Studies and Metropolitan Arts Press, Ltd), and the WAN Award in 2017, where the awards ceremony was held in London.

The practice was also a finalist in the 2014 WAN Awards for T-House, the "house" of a T-shirt manufacturer in Nonthaburi, Thailand. Their The Power House of SCG project, a mechanical building in Bangkok, Thailand, was a finalist in the "Factory" and "Cantilever" categories of the 2015 Architizer Awards. EKAR Architects has also proudly taken home the second prize in the international 2004 "Be More Like a Child As You Get Older" competition, a competition about integrated communities for all ages, organized by The Association of Collegiate Schools of Architecture (ACSA), United States.

Founder **Ekaphap Duangkaew** is currently also a regular lecturer in institutions in Singapore, Malaysia, and Thailand.

Local Progressive—Thailand Contemporary Architecture

Jenchieh HUNG, Founding President, Chinese-Thai Research Studio; Founding Principal, HAS design and research; Adjunct Professor, Chulalongkorn University; Guest Editor, *Architecture Asia*
Kulthida SONGKITTIPAKDEE, Founding Principal, HAS design and research; Adjunct Professor, Chulalongkorn University; Guest Editor, *Architecture Asia*

Author Information
Jenchieh HUNG: hasinfom@gmail.com
Kulthida SONGKITTIPAKDEE: hasinfom@gmail.com

Abstract

After a long period of "modernization" in Thailand, which ceased in 1940, a construction wave swept through the country, erecting many different types of modern buildings, which included typical complexes, as well as stylized architectural examples. More obvious contemporary architectural aesthetics were initiated as a new wave of architecture. In the early days of this wave, Architects 49 Limited (A49), led by Nithi Sthapitanonda, began an exploration of regionalism in their work. Thai contemporary architecture has been in bloom since the beginning of the twenty-first century. This essay focuses on the contemporary architecture of Thailand in Southeast Asia. Specifically, it concentrates on the exploration of modernity, regionalism, and futurism in Thai architecture led by twelve architectural firms, whose founders were born from 1940 to 1980.

Keywords

Southeast Asia, Thai contemporary architecture, regionalism, Thai-ness, architectural ideology.

1. Indigenous vs International

Between 1945 and 1965, many Southeast Asian countries, including Indonesia, Vietnam, Malaysia, and Singapore successively achieved independence. During the long period of colonization, Western modernism directly influenced the architectural practices of many Southeast Asian countries, even non-colonized Thailand. At the end of the twentieth century, it took a different turn, with discussions about Third World art and architecture in Europe and the United States leading to deeper explorations of regionalist architecture. One such, and the most famous of which, was the forum hosted by the Aga Khan Award for Architecture in 1985 in Dhaka, the capital of Bangladesh, discussing the work of Kenneth Frampton and the well-known thesis, "Critical Regionalism," written by Alexander Tzonis and Liane Lefaivre.

Balkrishna Doshi, Charles Correa, and others spoke at the event, arguing that regionalism represented the general awakening of Asian countries following their rapid economic growth and urbanization, but that the forms of regionalism were very much varied, depending on the region. The panelists also believed that regionalism would eventually evolve into various practice forms in response to social change in the city in an orderly and sequential manner.

Modernism, at that time, was spreading quickly throughout many Southeast Asian countries. For example, Indonesian architect Han Awal, who returned from his studies in Germany, was very much influenced by modernism when designing Atma Jaya Catholic University in Jakarta, Indonesia, for the first Indonesian president, Ahmad Sukarno; Vietnamese architect Ngo Viet Thu, who had worked in France for many years, was also steered by modernism in his design of the Presidential Palace for the first president of South Vietnam, Ngo Dinh Diem. Both these buildings share common characteristics: They are symmetrical in geometry, showing a heavy and orderly Western aesthetic, and they are made of concrete instead of local wood or bamboo—as was the tradition then—to shape a modern spatial formal language; what's more, concrete also helps keep rain away, thereby satisfying the needs of shade, ventilation, and an arcade in a tropical climate.

The modernism movement was particularly popular in Thailand. Plan Architect, founded by Paisarn Ratanawanakul in 1975, constructed Baiyoke Sky Tower in Bangkok, which is not only Thailand's tallest landmark, but which also symbolizes the end of the Cold War in Southeast Asia in the 1980s and the modernization and commercialization of Thailand. This international trend of modernism was, however, halted in 1983 by the pioneering firm Architects 49 Limited (A49), led by Nithi Sthapitanonda, with a new exploration of regionalism.

In the two brief years between 1986 and 1988, A49 completed the Architects 49 office and Muang Thai Life Assurance building and Phatra Insurance Auditorium. These works have shaped an architectural formal language, showing that modernity and indigenization are compatible with each other. A49 even took advantage of local projects as a medium for international export and shaped a brand-new perception of Thai architecture globally. They also released the firm album *Architects 49*, which was published by Images Publishing, were interviewed by Japan's *A+U Architecture and Urbanism Magazine*, and later published *A49 Progressive Vernacular*, which successfully shaped the world's perception of Thailand's locality, modernity, and culture. The Asian Financial Crisis in 1997, however, pushed Thai architecture to a new level and transformed it into a watershed, due to the influence of internal politics and external economic bubbles.

2. The Awakening Regionalism

The Asian Financial Crisis of 1997 hit the Thai economy tremendously and triggered a fundamental shift in the architecture industry. The first effect was the emergence of many independent architectural studios. With tens of thousands of companies in Thailand going bankrupt, and over 2.7 million unemployed, Thailand's leading architectural firms, including A49 and Plan Architect, were significantly affected. Most employees left large corporations to start their own small architectural studios. After leaving A49, Duangrit Bunnag founded Duangrit Bunnag Architect Limited (DBALP) in the wake of the Asian Financial Crisis in 1998, and completed the spectacular Costa Lanta Krabi Resort and Spa in Krabi, Thailand, in 2002. The project broke away from the traditional Thai resort/lodge model with a pioneering design steered toward respect for the natural environment and the tropical landscape, using local materials instead of the typical heavy double-sloped roof, symmetrical space layout, and decorative louvers. Therefore, it successfully created a new Thai-style resort with an emphasis on "feel." After leaving Plan Architect, Jeravej Hongsakul founded his firm IDIN Architects, which completed Phuket Gateway in 2007. The iconic building constructs a 100-meter promenade using local materials and concrete. On account of featuring natural elements, it also successfully creates an ecological plane of light, rain, and breeze.

Secondly, religious architecture and social residences rose in number. The Asian Financial Crisis affected Thai people for nearly ten years, and it was not until 2008 that global finance gradually returned to its pre-crisis level. During the years of hardship, the Thai government's two-pronged approach provided a salve by leading the belief of the Thai people, stabilizing society with Buddhism, the origin of spiritual peace for the Thai people, and building housing. Walllasia, founded by Suriya Umpansiriratana in 1998, constructed Wat Khao Buddhakodom temple in 1999, as well as a series of monks' dormitories, including the Buddhist Retreat and the Walled Monk's Cell. At the other end of their efforts, the government also gave permission for building social residences to improve the living standards of slums and communities. Community Architects for Shelter and Environment (CASE), founded in 1996 by Patama Roonrakwit—who is dedicated to slum rehabilitation, social residences, and post-disaster architecture— built TEN House in Bangkok and improved the quality of life in community housing.

Third, local materials and techniques were applied innovatively. In order to reduce the aftermath of the Asian Financial Crisis, the Thai government no longer relied on massive imports of its economy as it had done in the past, but instead strove to upgrade domestic industries. A series of industries, such as processing production, exquisite manufacturing, and tourism services were initiated, which also promoted the local development of the architecture industry. For instance, Bangkok Project Studio, founded by Boonserm Premthada in 2003, constructed Kantana Film and Animation Institute. Built with 600,000 hand-fired red bricks, the project not only brought employment to more than 100 bricklayers in two surrounding villages, but also presented local materials in a new light, through a new type of visual effect created with undulating walls that broke from the traditional red brick technique.

Figure 1
Nurse Dormitory,
Chulalongkorn Memorial
Hospital

Figure 2
Sarnsara Learning Center

Fourth, Thai-ness space was highlighted. Given that the government was committed to the combination of tourism and commerce, shopping malls and resort hotels were constructed on a grand scale in Thailand. Unlike the symbolic expressions of space of early architects such as Sumet Jumsai na Ayudhya and Rangsan Torsuwan, most of these malls and resorts were innovative and based on traditional space types with complex functions. The Commons Thonglor in Bangkok, designed by Department of ARCHITECTURE Co., which was co-founded by Amata Luphaiboon and Twitee Vajrabhaya Teparkum in 2004, is a good example. Inspired by the traditional Thai hammock, the practice rose the height of the whole building to create a large area with shade, ventilation, and an arcade. The Commons Thonglor not only reverses the traditional concept of the ground-floor commercial space, but also presents Thai-ness architecture in a modern way, in response to the city and climate.

In the decade from 1997 to 2007, as Thailand endured and recovered from the Asian Financial Crisis and the economy began to take off again, a wave of innovation was set off, led by Duangrit Bunnag, Boonserm Premthada, Patama Roonrakwit, Suriya Umpansiriratana, and Amata Luphaiboon, who were born in the 1960s. Their works were distinct from those of the first generation of Thai architects, who only presented expressions and aesthetics after returning from studies in Europe and the United States. In their works, their personal philosophical criticism and architectural theories are clearly retained, while combining Thailand's tropical geography and technological level, and highlighting sustainability at the same time. This new generation of architects, therefore, enable architecture to be less dependent on equipment, while strengthening the

emphasis on green, public, and urban interfaces, profoundly influencing the next group of architects.

3. Thai Architecture in Full Bloom

In 2008, with the prevalence of the internet, international architecture media such as *ArchDaily* and *Architizer* began to make wide tracks and take the world by storm. This resulted in more personal and critical architectural forms and formal spatial language gradually emerging, thus driving questions like "What is architecture?" and "How should architecture be done?" to be raised early in the design process. This showed that the focus of Thai architectural practices had shifted, from being merely about standard construction procedures to also thinking about how to help Thai architecture establish a better connection to society and culture. The twelve different types of architecture selected for this issue are typical examples, and include the projects Nurse Dormitory Chulalongkorn Memorial Hospital (Figure 1), Sarnsara Learning Center (Figure 2), SYC Office (Figure 3, page 11), No Sunrise No Sunset Pavilion (Figure 4, page 11), Elephant World (Figure 5, page 11), The Commons Saladaeng (Figure 6, page 11), Keeree Tara Riverside (Figure 7, page 12), PANNAR Sufficiency Economic and Agriculture Learning Center (Figure 8, page 12), Duriflex Warehouse (Figure 9, page 12), Radial House (Figure 10, page 12), Livist Resort Petchabun (Figure 11, page 13), and Pusayapuri Hotel (Figure 12, page 13).

These projects show that Thailand's contemporary architecture is much more diverse than its collection of popularly known tourist and commercial buildings. And many of these architecture, such as Nurse Dormitory Chulalongkorn Memorial Hospital—a cultural

10

tribute to the royal family, the Elephant Museum—a symbol for the care of natural ecology, the PANNAR Sufficiency Economic and Agriculture Learning Center—which honors disadvantaged industrial groups, and the Duriflex Warehouse—which reflects on practical industrial buildings, demonstrate the shift in the exploration of Thai contemporary architecture from form, space, and architecture to the complex disciplines of ecology, humanities, society, and industry.

Another steering factor was the government's promotion and emphasis of the primary industry—tourism—accelerating the development of creative tourism and eco-conservation related activities, in conjunction with the unique ecological, topographical, and advantageous tropical climatic of the country. This has not only led to the development of buildings in remote areas outside Bangkok, but has also spurred media coverage and public attention, contributing to the preservation and redevelopment of the culture of many regions in Thailand. As examples are Sarnsara Learning Center in Phetchaburi—famous for hand-fired red bricks, No Sunrise No Sunset Pavilion—where people are able to meditate with the landscape in Krabi, Elephant World—which is all about elephant conservation in Suvarnabhumi, and Livist Resort Petchabun—a simple yet natural resort with local plants and rough concrete. Though located in little-known places in Thailand, these projects build a unique sense of cultural identity, as well as help form self-confidence for the local residents by reflecting unique social resources and environmental phenomena through their architecture.

The establishment of the Thailand Creative Design Center (TCDC) at the beginning of the twenty-first century is also significant. A series of exhibitions on new materials were held at the center and nearly 60,000 books on architecture, art, textiles, and fashion were introduced. On the one hand, the center has diverted public attention toward traditional Thai aesthetics, and on the other, it has enriched the role of handicrafts in Thai contemporary architecture. For example, the roof of Keeree Tara Riverside by IDIN Architects is made of wooden panels designed by local artisans using traditional wood craftsmanship methods. It shows a balance between local aesthetics and modern forms, and presents brand new spatial effects. Also, Pusayapuri Hotel uses both red bricks and stones to echo the long history of Thailand's ancient pagodas. On top of that, decorative elements common to religious architecture have also been applied to the building's façade, forming a unique Thai aesthetic. However, both projects were designed in 2013 and were not completed until 2022, reflecting a ten-year break in the exploration of traditional aesthetics and craftsmanship in Thai architecture.

Finally, Thai-ness is being disseminated and popularized in society. The general public, too, seems to be very interested in Thai-ness, as evidenced by exhibitions, books, and institutions, such as the 2011 ASA Architect Expo organized by The Association of Siamese Architects under Royal Patronage (ASA) on the theme "Unlocking Thai Identity (*Plod Lock Ekaluck Thai*)" and Pracha Suweeranon's book *Thai Identity: From Thai to Thai Thai* (*Attaluck Thai: Chak Thai Soo Thai Thai*) (sameskybooks, Bangkok, 2011) published the same year. The 2012 Cool Thai (*Thai Tay*) exhibition at the Bangkok Art and Cultural Center also presented contemporary Thai-ness as a phenomenon in art and culture. But none more so than Department of ARCHITECTURE Co.'s The Commons Saladaeng and Stu/D/O Architects' Radial House, both completed in 2020. Both projects attempt to capture the

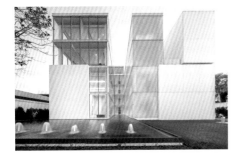

Figure 3
SYC Office

Figure 4
No Sunrise No Sunset
Pavilion

Figure 5
Elephant World

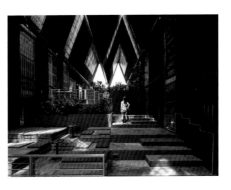

Figure 6
The Commons
Saladaeng

11

Figure 7
Keeree Tara Riverside

essence of Thai-ness by conveying a spiritual identity through form, architecture, and materials. On the one hand, they share an open space on the first floor of the building, and on the other, they echo the multifunctional *tai toon* of traditional Thai houses, which refers to a composite space that can be used for communicating and activities. Therefore, both abstractly convey the perceptual use and aesthetic development of Thai-ness in architecture.

4. Conclusion

After the end of colonization, Southeast Asian countries such as Indonesia, Vietnam, Malaysia, Singapore, and even non-dominated Thailand were uniformly influenced by Europe and the United States and steered toward modernism, adopting national symbols. However, Oscar Niemeyer's work in Brazil in the mid-twentieth century—especially the free forms of concrete applied to the construction of shade, stairs, and structures—differed from the rigid geometry of early modernist architecture. They deeply influenced many Southeast Asian countries in their individual pursuit of a "new" sense of independence, though within the same tropical climate.

Thailand's economic prosperity spawned a variety of creative industries, as its religious beliefs shaped Thai purity and optimism and its tropical climate nurtured abundant natural resources. And that is why, when Thai architects were appointed to assignments different from traditional political mandates, such as animal conservation buildings, meditation spaces, agricultural exhibition centers, and eco-resorts, they were able to design these buildings independent of political factors, resulting in them featuring a tropical, regional, and spatial exploration different

Figure 8
PANNAR Sufficiency Economic and Agriculture Learning Center

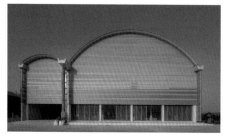

Figure 9
Duriflex Warehouse

Figure 10
Radial House

12

Figure 11
Livist Resort Petchabun

Figure 12
Pusayapuri Hotel

from that of other Southeast Asian countries, thereby establishing the unique typology of Thai contemporary architecture.

Adding to that, Thailand also developed a rich historical, culture, and craft aesthetics, which are reflected in its architectural design, and which have had lasting influence. For example, Nithi Sthapitanonda, born in the 1940s, through A49 created a series of buildings with a distinct tropical Thai aesthetic that has influenced architects born later, such as Duangrit Bunnag (born in the 1960s), Rachaporn Choochuey, (born in the 1970s), and Apichart Srirojanapinyo, Chanasit Cholasuek, Patchara Wongboonsin, and Ekaphap Duangka, (born in the 1980s). These architects form a genealogical tree of local Thai architects.

Beyond these things, Thailand has also developed a universal model of architectural practice in spite of the different social contexts arising from the long-term gap between the rich and the poor. For example, due to limited urban resources and a rising population, the government approved the social housing project at the beginning of the twentieth century and created open spaces; recently, a mass of slums was rehabilitated and the government introduced the concept of pocket parks. These projects not only address the housing needs of low-income households, but also create sustainable urban ecological spaces and develop a set of solutions to social problems. To that end, Vin Varavarn Architects (VVA) came up with a systemic strategy of educating local farm workers to take advantage of vernacular materials as inexpensive and versatile materials by themselves.

A Buddhist country for more than 2,000 years, Thailand showcases the wisdom of Asian architecture through multiple aspects: a humble sense of autonomy, peaceful design strategy, and sustainable ecological construction, all of which have been

represented by the work of the twelve architectural practices featured in this issue—Plan Architect, Architects 49 Limited (A49), Duangrit Bunnag Architect Limited (DBALP), Walllasia, Bangkok Project Studio, Department of ARCHITECTURE Co., IDIN Architects, Vin Varavarn Architects (VVA), all(zone), Stu/D/O Architects, Patchara + Ornnicha Architects (POAR), and EKAR Architects. Less than a century after the independence of other Southeast Asian countries, Thailand, which has never been colonized, has shown such richness in the Southeast Asian architectural language, in response to different social contexts. It is not only an exploration of the region, but also a guide for European, American, and Asian architects toward a new future amid the challenges of global climate crises and environmental change.

Figure Credits
Figure 1: Nurse Dormitory Chulalongkorn Memorial Hospital (courtesy of Plan Architect: Nitisak Chobdamrongtham, Apichai Apichatanon, and Wara Jithpratuck).
Figure 2: Sarnsara Learning Center (courtesy of Architects 49 Limited: Prabhakorn Vadanyakul and Somkiat Lochindapong).
Figure 3: SYC Office (courtesy of Duangrit Bunnag Architect Limited: Duangrit Bunnag).
Figure 4: No Sunrise No Sunset Pavilion (courtesy of Walllasia: Suriya Umpansiriratana).
Figure 5: Elephant World (courtesy of Bangkok Project Studio: Boonserm Premthada).
Figure 6: The Commons Saladaeng (courtesy of Department of ARCHITECTURE: Amata Luphaiboon and Twitee Vajrabhaya Teparkum).
Figure 7: Keeree Tara Riverside (courtesy of IDIN Architects: Jeravej Hongsakul).
Figure 8: PANNAR Sufficiency Economic and Agriculture Learning Center (courtesy of Vin Varavarn Architects: M. L. Varudh Varavarn).
Figure 9: Duriflex Warehouse (courtesy of all (zone): Rachaporn Choochuey).
Figure 10: Radial House (courtesy of Stu/D/O Architects: Apichart Srirojanapinyo).
Figure 11: Livist Resort Petchabun (courtesy of Patchara + Ornnicha Architecture: Patchara Wongboonsin and Ornnicha Duriyaprapan).
Figure 12: Pusayapuri Hotel (courtesy of EKAR Architects: Ekaphap Duangkaew).

Bangkok Bastards, Rural Crossbreeds, and Indigenous Hybrids—CHAT Architects' Documentation of Thailand's Living Typologies, Urbanism, and Ecologies

Chatpong **CHUENRUDEEMOL**, Principal Architect, CHAT Architects, Thailand

Abstract

In 2012, Chat Architects initiated their "Bangkok Bastards" project, an on-going documentation of everyday architecture, created by everyday people, to solve everyday problems in Bangkok, the capital of Thailand. The research subjects of this project range from living shantytowns to moving food carts, and temporary construction workers' houses to the now abandoned curtained love motels—in essence, misfit architectures that Bangkokians encounter on a daily basis, but view as insignificant eyesores to the city.

Through richly rendered plans, sections, elevations, and isometrics—which are colorful, tactile, and messy, rather than monotone, minimal, and clean—Chat Architects tells the story of grassroots design ingenuity, opportunistic adaptations, and the humorous spirit of Bangkok's underprivileged and "unseen" populations, as seen through the lens of these beautiful "bastards." Over recent years, the research boundary has moved from Bangkok and out into the Thai countryside, where "Rural Crossbreeds" reveal bastard agricultural buildings, pavilions, and contraptions that are rooted in Thailand's widely spread, long-standing cultivation of rice. The research has since moved beyond the rice paddies and fruit farms in the region, called Isaan, into the isolated forests and mountains of Thailand to also identify "Indigenous Hybrids" that reveal the inventive spirit embodied in the Karen hill tribe population in Ratchaburi Province.

Author Information
Chatpong CHUENRUDEEMOL: cchuenrudeemoll@hotmail.com

Keywords

Bangkok Bastards, Rural Crossbreeds, Indigenous Hybrids, everyday architecture, local adaptation/improvization.

Figure 1
A front door bridge in Dusit
District, Bangkok, Thailand

In 2012, Chat Architects initiated a design research project referred to as "Bangkok Bastards." It began with a desire to discover how daily life, local conditions, and human (not theoretical) responses to everyday problems in Bangkok could lead to authentic design strategies that were adapted to life in the many neighborhoods of Bangkok, Thailand. We weren't interested in deriving a universal strategy, proclaiming a paradigm shift, or creating new Thai typologies. We simply wanted to create an architecture, piece of furniture, or an urban strategy that was rooted in authentic, specific, (many times hidden) local conditions. We wanted to learn to "grow" designs that are relevant, empathetic, and relatable to Bangkokians.

Over the course of ten years, as our projects and curiosity expanded from Bangkok to the city's urban peripheries, the scope our "Bastard" research naturally grew to include the documentation of "Rural Crossbreeds," which are various Bastard countryside architecture. In particular, we were drawn to Thailand's northeast region, Isaan, the country's agricultural epicenter and most under-developed region. Here, we documented not only Bastard buildings, but homemade objects, hacked vehicles, hidden festivals, and hybrid ecologies inherently tied to Thailand's unique culture of rice farming and cultivation.

Our experience with agricultural ecologies recently, again, led us on another path, to the forest peripheries and mountain landscapes that surround Thailand's rice paddies. Residing within these untouched natural regions, we found the *chao kao*, the indigenous hill tribes of Thailand. As Thailand's rapid development and burgeoning cities eat away at the *chao kao*'s forest and mountain habitats, we see how the increasing social, economic, and political pressures placed upon Thailand's stateless people have resulted in rampant, but unspoken injustice, prejudice, and poverty. While woeful on the one hand, on the other, the *chao kao*'s plights of desperation have inspired indigenous hill tribe communities to not only preserve valuable age-old customs and practices, but also forced them to imagine, invent, and develop new "Indigenous Hybrids," which allow them to cope with modern-day problems.

1. Bangkok Bastards

Bangkok Bastards refer to homegrown architectural concoctions created by everyday people to solve everyday problems in everyday life. The "Bastards" may include a rundown shack in a neighborhood *chum chon* (slum), a local street vendor cart, a bastardized shophouse, or a make-shift sidewalk bench. Bangkokians walk past Bastards every day, but would never consider them as serious design or architecture.

Like its human namesake, an architectural bastard has no traceable architectural parents/lineage, no cultural history, and no design theory that legitimizes it form. Many view Bastards as eyesores to the city, lacking in any serious design pedigree, and being unworthy of serious documentation or research. However, we argue that Bangkok Bastards are the most authentically inventive examples of architecture in Thailand. They are pure, intuitive, flexible, humorous responses to real problems. Oftentimes, their strategies utilize cheap, salvaged, discarded materials, that have been hacked, re-imagined, and repurposed in entirely new and unexpected ways. They take advantage of existing urban conditions and turn them upside down to create a new way of living, selling, and playing in the city.

15

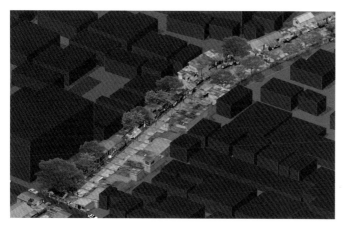

Figure 2
Klong Peng Chumchon, a
"*dead klong*" community in
Thonglor Neighborhood,
Bangkok, Thailand

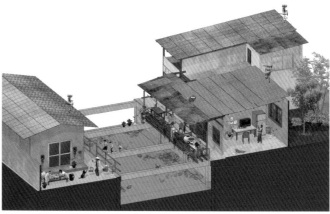

Figure 3
Hybrid bridge beam—
section of a canal and
waterside residence
showing unique concrete
canal beams that keep the
canal's retaining wall from
crumbling into the water.
These infrastructural beams
have been repurposed by
locals as "community
bridges;" children expertly
scamper across these
slender members above the
putrid waters.

Bangkok Bastards are "live." They are not historical case studies that are frozen in time, and which have been documented to preserve a past. Bastards are dynamic, living, architectural and spatial strategies that are constantly evolving—yearly, monthly, weekly, and daily. They are architecture that one sees, experiences, and engages with immediately when stepping onto the streets, alleys, or shanties of Bangkok.

In historic Bangkok, once known as the Venice of the East, wooden houses on stilts that lined the city's countless canals were fronted by front door boat landings, which welcomed visitors arriving by boat. As the aquatic city modernized, boat traffic along the canals eventually gave way to surface street networks and automotive traffic. A new Bastard, the front door bridge (Figure 1, page 15), replaced the traditional front door boat landing as the new front door to the canal-facing homes. This new Bastard typology connects waterside residences to the new urban infrastructure, like the urban street and pedestrian sidewalk. The bridge's trademark is its stepped arch form that allows the occasional boat to pass underneath. The gesture also succeeds in lifting each footbridge to an elevated and dignified position, announcing the presence of the old waterside residence to the modern street. Prem Prachakon Canal's front door bridges are unique for their multicolored front doors, with their radiating burglar proofing that adorn each door like porcupine quills. Cantilevered benches overlooking the canal allow residents to enjoy a new eco-urban lifestyle.

Just about a century ago, Bangkok was filled with networks of endless *klongs*, or canals, which supplied water to the city's abundant rice fields and fruit orchards. With the arrival of automobiles, these vibrant waterways have

Figure 4
Street food mansion,
Dusit District, Bangkok,
Thailand

Figure 5
Rendition of the street food
mansion in Dusit District

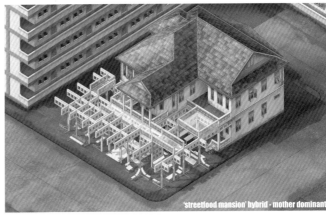

'streetfood mansion' hybrid - mother dominant

Figure 6
"Bastardizing the
Bastard"—"Bastard child" 1

mostly been topped over with asphalt. However, a few "dead *klong*" communities still remain. One of these historic communities, the Klong Peng Chumchon (Figure 2, page 16), is ironically located among high-end homes, luxury condominiums, and chic shopping plazas in one of Bangkok's most affluent districts, Thonglor Neighborhood.

2. Bastardizing the Bastard

Bangkok Bastards have been documented not only for historical reference or the preservation of cultural knowledge. In "bastardizing the Bastard," we hack and transform the original Bastards into brand-new Bastards. In doing so, the DNA of the original—imbued with authentic socioeconomic, cultural, and tectonic identity—are naturally embedded into the new design. By combining newly imagined programs and imposing new constraints to the existing Bastards, we are able to propose realistic alternative futures for Bangkok that are rooted in the understanding of existing conditions.

Chat Architects continually engages in theoretical exercises in-house of "bastardizing the Bastard." These in-house experiments allow us to continually sharpen and fine-tune our Bastard design strategies, which have proven useful when engaged in client projects.

Hidden behind the Dusit Neighborhood Police Station and Dormitories stands a beautiful, yet unoccupied historic colonial mansion, whose original owners have passed away. Although empty, the structure is not neglected, as a local food vendor has assumed the role of informal caretaker, preventing thieves, burglars, and drug addicts from invading this historical property. In return, she has been

allowed to "bastardize" the front garden and existing veranda into an open-air restaurant that serves the local police force and their families. Umbrella stands, plastic stools, folding tables, and other street food furniture are crossbred with the tropical classical residence to become a new street food mansion (Figure 4, page 16).

In Figure 6, the more dominant characteristics of the "mother," the colonial mansion, is exhibited. The original colonnaded veranda structure with its classical columns, intricately casts ventilation panels; the classical balcony balustrade is "bastardized" to become a new hybrid space. The entire mansion is reimagined as a new bed-and-breakfast hotel with Bangkok-colonial open-air "dining rooms."

In Figure 7 (page 18), the traits of the "father," the street food restaurant, are assumed as dominant characteristics. Multicolored plastic stools, folding tables, and other informal furniture are crossbred with the original mansion to create a new food court and playground typology that are enjoyed by policemen's families residing in the adjacent dormitories.

In Thailand, most construction workers live on the actual construction site and are tasked with building their own temporary dormitory from leftover building materials found on-site. This particular CWH (construction workers' house) typology (Figure 8, page 18) is composed of two elements: the "core" and the "scaffolding." The "core" is a simple one- to two-story subdivided structure comprising small, hot, and poorly ventilated rooms sheathed in corrugated zinc sheets. What makes living here bearable is the "scaffolding," which works as a veranda-like circulation element that doubles as multipurpose outdoor living spaces for cooking, eating, drinking, washing/drying laundry, and socializing.

17

Figure 7
"Bastardizing the Bastard"—"Bastard child" 2

Figure 8
Construction workers' house, Rama 9 Road, Bangkok, Thailand

Figure 9
Samsen STREET Hotel by Chat Architects, Bangkok, Thailand

The Samsen STREET Hotel (Figure 9) involves the transformation (or "bastardization") of an existing curtained sex motel, one of Bangkok's long-standing "unspoken" typologies. A newly introduced "scaffolding" turns the existing curtained sex motel model inside out—formally and programmatically—by transforming the once introverted, dark, and secretive building with a socially questionable program into a new extroverted street hotel/hostel typology that stimulates and reactivates street life in this former red-light district. The two main components of the hotel's renovation can be clearly perceived. The existing building is refinished simply in plain gray polished cement plaster, while the new interventions come in the form of a pale green "living scaffolding," (a Bastard derivation of the construction workers' house scaffolding). There are three scaffolding elements: the "*soi*" (vertical alley and stage), the *rabeang* (sidewalk terrace), and the "*nahng glang plang*" (outdoor movie theater).

3. Rural Crossbreeds

Bastard architecture is prevalent not only in Bangkok, but also exists throughout the Thai countryside. These "Rural Crossbreeds" are inherently tied to the country's agricultural heritage. As Thailand is a rice nation, Bastard buildings, pavilions, and contraptions are constantly being invented and reinvented by Thailand's farmers to facilitate the planting, cultivation, and harvesting of rice. Hybrid rice villages are populated with architectural crossbreeds that combine urban shophouse typologies with rural Thai house-on-stilts variants. Interstate roads linking rice towns are likewise strewn with Bastards, such as

Figure 10
Street elevation of Samsen STREET Hotel by Chat Architects showing the introduction of green "living scaffolding" elements to the existing concrete structure. The vertical "soi" (vertical alley) scaffolding allows utility workers to service all MEP systems exposed on the façade

Figure 11
Samsen STREET Hotel at night—the green "soi" scaffolding transforms into a vertical stage on weekends and holidays, allowing for public street concerts to re-energize this once dilapidated red-light neighborhood

Figure 12
Garlic-drying shed in a plantation in Mae Faag Province, northern Thailand

roadside pop-up vegetable stands with homemade expressway billboards positioned precariously close to speeding traffic.

In some instances, unique timber and bamboo structural systems have also been tailored in garlic and onion plantations to serve as hanging infrastructure for drying garlic and red onion (Figure 12), as the roots of these produce must remain dry, mold-free, and away from the moist ground. A large corridor cuts through the middle of the shed, wide enough for a medium-size vehicle to drive through for delivery and pickup. During drying season, beige and purple clouds of garlic and red onion seemingly float in the 6-meter-tall interior as their unique aromas fill the air.

Figure 14 (page 20) reveals the section of a brick kiln shed of Sookthawee Brick Suppliers who fire local red bricks for the Nakhon Si Thammarat community. The two main architectural components are the large brick kiln constructed of the very bricks that they are firing, and the giant Bastard shed canopy that has been constructed of salvaged timber, which protects the brick production zones from the elements.

In Figure 16 (page 21), a narrow 2-meter stretch of grass surrounding a flood reservoir is "colonized" by a local restaurant to make for a most unique eating area. A circular road bisects the restaurant into two parts: the kitchen and food preparation area lies on the sunken landward side of the road, while the dining area with scenic views of the water is located on the elevated grassy perimeter that encircles the reservoir. Food servers precariously cross the road, dodging traffic, to deliver the hot dishes to customers who wait under the umbrella dining tents.

With cartoon beach towels as privacy screen to shield from adjacent traffic, street food umbrellas for overhead shade, and cheap vinyl mats as simple picnic ground cover, this homemade

tent architecture makes the most of mundane materials to create a unique waterside dining experience.

Rod haer or the Morlum parade truck (Figure 18, page 21), is the embodiment of *sanuk* (fun) in Thailand's northeastern Isaan culture. This concert-on-wheels is the modern version of the traditional *kabuoen haer*, which is a village parade on foot that takes place when family and friends in an Isaan village collectively celebrate important occasions, such as a wedding or a monk's ordination, by dancing, singing, and parading through the local streets. Many times, the preferred background music is Morlum, the lively local Isaan folk music.

Maha Sarakahm Village (Figure 19, page 22) is a prototypical *moo bahn* or small town in Thailand's northeastern Isaan. The buildings that line the main road of the town are the architectural offsprings of the urban shophouse and the traditional wooden Thai stilt house, which is commonly found in rice paddies that encircle the town.

4. Indigenous Hybrids

The indigenous people of Thailand were formed by ethnic minority groups who migrated to the mountainous regions of northern Thailand from China, Laos, and Myanmar. For centuries, Thailand's hill tribe population, known as *chao kao*, lived sustainably within their secluded natural habitats, practicing traditional crop-rotation farming techniques, cultivating small scale livestock, and gathering food provided by the bounties of the forest and mountains. In the first half of the twentieth century, they were largely left to their agrarian way of life and largely isolated from mainstream society. However, as

19

Figure 13
Garlic drying sheds located
at the heart of garlic and
onion plantations are a
common sight in northern
Thailand

Figure 14
A brick kiln Bastard in
Nakhon Si Thammarat,
southern Thailand

Figure 15
Brick kiln's building and
firing process

Workers begin arranging fresh clay blocks in
kiln

Workers stack bricks to create arched firewood
"tunnels" at base of pile

Bricks stacked to the top of kiln wall, one side
at a time

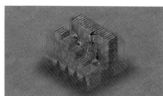

Bricks stacked in stepped piles to allow workers
to access the top of the piles

Bricks completely filled to top of kiln

Workers insert firewood into arched tunnels to
begin firing the bricks, ensuring that firewood
is arranged throughout the entire length of the
tunnels in order to distribute the heat evenly at
bottom of brick pile

As bricks are fired, intense smoke and heat is
released through the pile, and out from the top
of the pile

When the firing of the bricks is complete, the
bricks are left to cool before being loaded onto
trucks for delivery. At this stage, the newly fired
bricks and the brick kiln appear as one
monolithic earthen mass, and it can be seen
that the brick kiln shell is poetically
constructed of the same bricks that are being
fired from within its walls

Figure 16
Umbrella restaurant, Surin
Province, northeastern
Thailand

modern life and urban development began to infringe upon the country's once remote forest and mountain regions, and as governmental policies turned most of Thailand's natural landscapes into national parks, the indigenous populations were slowly pushed out of the nation's "protected" forests. Denied the right to Thai citizenship, the indigenous people are unable to own property or become legally employed, in addition to being treated as criminals who "invaded" the nation's forests and mountains. Unable to sustain their traditional way of life, the *chao kao* have long endured a life of extreme poverty, injustice, and discrimination. Caught between two worlds, the indigenous people of Thailand are faced with the challenge and struggle of assimilating into modern society, and are at the same time also trying to preserve their valuable cultural heritage.

4.1 *Chao Kao*

The *chao kao*—or people of hill tribes—settled in the mountains in northern Thailand several hundred years ago and they include the Karen, Akha, Hmong, Lahu, Lisu, Mien, and Palaung tribes. Since the times of their ancestors, they have practiced a slash-and-burn method of subsistence farming, mixing rice and other crops in hybrid plots to constantly circulate nutrients in the soil. In the 1950s, popular misperception about the destructive nature of controlled slash-and-burn agriculture, compounded with the increasing fear of insurgency and rapid deforestation due to modernization, led the government to exert greater control on hill tribe populations. Despite the overwhelming challenges, the hill tribes of Thailand struggle to preserve their way of life and their physical and spiritual connections to the forest and mountain landscape, which are manifested as "Indigenous Hybrids," which

Figure 17
View of the umbrella restaurant's dining area facing the picturesque flood reservoir

Figure 18
Rod haer (Morlum parade truck), northeastern Thailand

Figure 19
Anatomy of an Isaan
Village—Maha Sarakham
Village, northeastern
Thailand

Figure 20
A Karen tribe farmer in Suan
Peung, Ratchaburi Province,
Thailand

define authentic and inventive local tribal crafts, architecture,
and ecologies.

4.2 Karen Hill Tribe

The Karen are the largest indigenous hill tribe ethnic minority in
Thailand, numbering close to 1,000,000. They are believed to be
descendants of Sino-Tibetan speaking people who once settled in
China near the Gobi Desert, but whose majority now reside in
Kayin State in Myanmar. Many Karen people have migrated to
northern Thailand, settling mostly in refugee camps along the
Thai-Myanmar border regions. Their status as refugees bars them
from leaving the hillside refugee camps in which they reside. As
non-Thai citizens, Karen people find little employment opportunities
outside the camps and risk getting arrested by the police if they
are caught engaged in illegal employment in mainstream Thai
society. Many Karen people who reside in the refugee camps or as
"homeless" nomads in remote hillside forest locations still practice
the traditional agrarian way of life, based on their unique crop-
rotational plantations.

Figure 21
A Karen bamboo house on
stilts, Suan Peung,
Ratchaburi Province,
Thailand

The Karen *tieng na* (Figure 22) is a small, elevated, open-air
pavilion located at the edge of a rice paddy. It is used as a
temporary shelter from the elements by farmers while they work in
the fields during the day. Karen people have also devised a unique
mobile T-shirt scarecrow system to scare away pests. From the
shaded comfort of the *tieng na*, a farmer can chase away birds
with a simple tug of a string that animates all the scarecrows
throughout the entire plot.

Figure 22
A Karen *tieng na*, Suan
Peung, Ratchaburi Province,
Thailand

The communal seed-mixing ceremony is usually carried
out in the *tieng na*. Karen farmers use bamboo tube

Figure 23
A Karen bamboo mixed-seed
dispenser

Figure 24
The Karen way of rotational
farming

dispensers (Figure 23) to mix and introduce a variety of seeds into their plots, along with rice grains. This seed mix produces a variety of plants, like sesame, gourd, squash, and chillis, which help maintain the health of the soil and sustain nutrients within it. Floral seeds that produce cosmos, marigold, and cockscomb flowers are also introduced to divert the attention of insects from the edible plants to the flowers' sweet nectar.

The Karen tribe practices a unique rotational farming system (Figure 24) that involves the planting of different crops in the same plot of land in order to maintain the health of the soil, sustain soil nutrients, and control weed and pest infestations. An outer farm ring is planted with pumpkin, gourd, cassava, and beans, which are feasted on by pests, which then become too full to eat the contents of the inner plot. A simple manual tug-and-pull T-shirt scarecrow system also helps to scare away flying pests like birds, who come by to peck away at the crop.

Figure Credits
Figure 1: A front door bridge (author's image).
Figure 2: Klong Peng Chumchon, a dead *klong* community in Thonglor Neighborhood, Bangkok, Thailand (author's image).
Figure 3: Hybrid bridge beam (author's image).
Figure 4: Street food mansion in Dusit District, Bangkok, Thailand (author's photo).
Figure 5: Rendition of street food mansion in Dusit District, Bangkok, Thailand (author's image).
Figure 6: "Bastardizing the Bastard"—"Bastard child" 1 (author's image).
Figure 7: "Bastardizing the Bastard"—"Bastard child" 2 (author's image).
Figure 8: Construction workers' house, Rama 9 Road, Bangkok, Thailand (author's image).
Figure 9: Samsen STREET Hotel by CHAT Architects, Bangkok, Thailand (author's image).
Figure 10: Street elevation of Samsen STREET Hotel by CHAT Architects (author's image).
Figure 11: Samsen STREET Hotel at night (author's photo).
Figure 12: Garlic drying shed in a plantation in Mae Faag Province, northern Thailand (author's image).
Figure 13: Garlic drying sheds located at the heart of garlic and onion plantations are a common sight in northern Thailand (author's image).
Figure 14: Brick kiln "Bastard," Nakhon Si Thamarat, southern Thailand (author's image).
Figure 15: Brick kiln's building and firing process (author's image).
Figure 16: Umbrella restaurant, Surin Province, northeastern Thailand (author's image).
Figure 17: View of the umbrella restaurant's dining area facing the picturesque flood reservoir (author's photo).
Figure 18: Rod haer (Morlum parade truck), northeast Thailand (author's image).
Figure 19: Anatomy of an Isaan Village—Maha Sarakham Village, northeastern Thailand (author's image).
Figure 20: A Karen farmer in Suan Peung, Ratchaburi Province, Thailand (author's photo).
Figure 21: A Karen bamboo house on stilts, Suan Peung, Ratchaburi Province, Thailand (author's image).
Figure 22: A Karen *tieng na*, Suan Peung, Ratchaburi Province, Thailand (author's image).
Figure 23: A Karen bamboo mixed-seed dispenser, Suan Peung, Ratchaburi Province, Thailand (author's image).
Figure 24: The Karen way of rotational farming (author's image).

Modernization and Localization: Modern Architectural Education in Thailand, 1930s–1950s

Chomchon FUSINPAIBOON, Assistant Professor, Chulalongkorn University, Thailand; Co-Founder, DRFJ (Design & Research by Fusinpaiboon & Jang), Thailand

Abstract

Modernization and localization, as well as the question of where the point of good balance between the two is, have long been important issues in Asian architecture. This article explores these issues through a critical examination of modern architectural education in Thailand from the 1930s to the 1950s—when both the modern practice of and training in architecture were formally established—and demonstrates a hybrid nature of these issues in theoretical, practical, and geographical aspects. With archival materials as evidence, it is revealed how Western architectural theories with Beaux-Arts roots (hailing from France, England, Belgium, and the United States) were hybridized in Thailand, along local constraints, within the cultural, political, and economic contexts of the country's "nation building" period. The article also highlights out how the English Arts and Crafts ideology helped to appropriate modernism in Thai postwar context. Modern architectural education in Thailand during this period proves the complexity of the concept of modernity and locality in architecture.

Author Information

Chomchon FUSINPAIBOON: chomchon.f@chula.ac.th

Keywords

Modernization, localization, architectural education, hybridization, modern Asian architecture.

A PERSPECTIVE VIEW OF A SEASIDE HOTEL

Figure 1
A studio work of the Faculty of Architecture at Chulalongkorn University, created between 1939 and 1941

1. Introduction

A formal and modern architectural education, at an advanced and higher certification level, was established in Thailand in 1933 with the formation of the Faculty of Architecture in Chulalongkorn University, Bangkok, Thailand. Throughout its almost three decades of early development, it went through challenges, from making sense of Europe's Beaux-Arts principles of architecture within Thailand's "nation building" context before World War II, to adapting it—with an English Arts and Crafts twist—to accommodate international modernism and Thai tradition in the immediate postwar period.

2. Thailand's First School of Architecture

The origin and early development of the Faculty of Architecture in Chulalongkorn University in the 1930s show similarities with the establishment of several architecture schools before World War II in Asia, such as in Japan and China. These schools provided architectural training for Asian students, so that they no longer needed to travel to Europe or the United States to study architecture. They formed part of the establishment of a modern architecture culture in the region, engaging in the interaction between modernity—perceived as deriving from the West—and the traditions of local cultures. Their curriculums, students' projects, and buildings, as well as the works built by teachers and graduates, embraced both modern architectural principles and traditional characteristics derived from the studies of the historical monuments and vernacular architecture of Asia.

In the late-nineteenth century, after Siam (later named Thailand in 1939) opened to global economy because of the pressures of Western imperial powers, the construction industry and jobs within the industry were dominated by foreigners, who constituted mainly of European architects and Chinese contractors and builders. Prior to the 1932 Siamese revolution in Thailand that put the Thai monarchy under a constitution, the royal government had produced a plan to promote construction education at all levels, so that more locals rather than foreigners could be employed in jobs within the construction industry. This plan by the royal government paralleled the mindset of Luang Sukkhawatthanasunthon, a prominent engineer, who was of the opinion that the Thai labor force was just as good as the Chinese migrant labor force for many kinds of work, but because they lacked proper training, it allowed the domination of the Chinese.[1] He made this observation during the construction of the Memorial Bridge across the Chao Phraya River to expand Bangkok's urban areas, which was one of the major projects initiated by the last reign of absolute monarchy.

The royal government's plan succeeded, along with many of their other plans, that were initiated after the 1932 revolution and steered toward modernization. These plans were prioritized by the new government under the People's Party, for the acceleration of modernization to build a new Thai nation that was meant to be different from the one under the old regime; it included establishing vocational construction schools nationwide, along with a special school that would offer studies for a more advanced level of construction training. The former would train carpenters, plasterers, and painters, with the aim of producing graduates who would be *chang khum ngan* and *chang ka ngan* (foremen), who would substitute *chin teng* (Chinese foremen). The first

25

construction school of this kind was Uthaen Thawai School, which was founded in 1933 in Bangkok.

The second type of school, which focused on higher education trained prospective architects for positions in the public sector. The main employers in this sector were the Department of Municipal Works and The Fine Arts Department, which were responsible for most of the state's construction works. These departments had previously been served mainly by Europeans, and only a limited number of Siamese architects who had graduated from Europe.[2] The government claimed that training at such an advanced level was already available at Po Chang School in Bangkok since 1930, and so in 1933, when Chulalongkorn University had a plan to expand, this advanced-level course to develop architects was transferred to the university from Po Chang School.[3] This move to create a specialized higher education to train architects aimed to lend prestige to architects and place them at the top of the construction team, completely differentiated from craftspeople, builders, and engineers.[4]

Chulalongkorn University's architect training courses began in the Faculty of Engineering on May 23, 1933, where subjects on structure were taught by professors from the Faculty of Engineering. One student who studied there at that time recalled that the subject on structure was very intense, actually equipping him to calculate the structure of a two-story building without an engineer's assistance.[5]

This training for architects became independently established as the Department of Architecture, following the issue of the Act of Chulalongkorn University BE 2477 on March 7, 1935.[6] Despite being established originally in the Faculty of Engineering, the three-year course was now oriented toward the artistic side of architecture rather than the scientific side of it (Figure 1, page 26, displays an example of a studio project). With foundational courses tailored to especially focus on classical architecture, the curriculum followed Beaux-Arts principles from Europe and the United States (Figure 2).[7] Most of the subjects mainly followed the curriculum of the School of Architecture of Liverpool University, United Kingdom, which was where Nat Phothiprasat, the founder of the Faculty of Architecture at Chulalongkorn University, had graduated from.

3. Localizing Measured Drawing

Although a heavy resemblance to Liverpool University's School of Architecture's course structure is observed, a more in-depth analysis reveals that some subjects functioned in a different way from their original versions from Liverpool University. In the university, the module "Measured Drawing" was taught by assigning students to do field work that consisted of measuring and drawing classical architecture. However, in Chulalongkorn University, the module was taught by measuring ancient Thai architecture, which did not provide an opportunity for students to be more familiar with Western classical building design, which their classes focused on. However, it did allow them to compensate for the lack of texts about Thai architecture in the classes.

Using skills learned from their surveying class, groups of students were tasked to measure a wide range of ancient Thai architecture, which included surviving buildings of earlier eras, such as the *prang* (pagoda) of Wat Ratchapradit, Bangkok, and Phra Pathom Chedi, Nakhon Pathom, and the ruins, such as Wat Phra Sri Sanphet in Ayutthaya, Prasat Hin Phimai, and Nakhon Ratchasima; they measured, sketched, and made drawings of

Figure 2
A work of Unchit Wasuwat, a student at Chulalongkorn University from 1939 to 1941, showing a composition of classical elements following Beaux-Arts principles

Figure 3
The measured works and reconstruction of an ancient monument showing Phra Prang Wat Phraram; by Unchit Wasuwat, a student at Chulalongkorn University from 1939 to 1941

พระปรางค์วัดพระราม

Figure 4
Faculty of Architecture
building at Chulalongkorn
University designed by
Lucien Coppé, 1941

these structures when they return to the university. In the case of ruins, where existing edifices were partly demolished, students needed to research contemporary styles found in other edifices and apply those styles to the drawings (Figure 3, page 26).[8] Therefore, the "Measured Works" module of the Department of Architecture at Chulalongkorn University also provided an exercise for students to reconstruct the lost architecture of the kingdom. This must have been perceived as good support for building up the knowledge and texts about traditional Thai architecture, which was still significantly unavailable at that time.

4. Localized Modernism?

While there were differences in the purpose between some subjects at Chulalongkorn and Liverpool Universities—despite them having the same name—the perception of their overall similarity, as well as the full curriculum of advanced subjects in Chulalongkorn University drew criticism, specifically on whether the modern curriculum was adequately localized to suit Thai context. Prominent Thai architect Mom Chao Itthithepsan Kridakorn, who had graduated from L' École Nationale Supérieure Des Beaux-Arts, Paris, France, argued that the curriculum was not responsive to the reality of the contemporary construction industry in Siam, in which the graduates of the school would be obliged to work.[9] An example was the teaching of construction by assigning students to copy construction drawings from foreign textbooks.

He commented that the curriculum should allow most students to be trained as vocational architects who would not have to take a long time to graduate, and who could work as employees in offices, mainly executing basic design and drafting. He claimed

that only a few of the students should be given the opportunity to study advanced subjects to graduate as professional architects and set up their own offices. He was, however, not positive in the necessity of the latter as the backward situation of the construction industry in Siam at that time reassured him that this would not happen soon. He insisted that the construction industry involving craftsmanship should be improved alongside architectural education; otherwise, graduates' ability to design architecture would be useless, as no one would be able to build them properly.

Another criticism came through the article "Sathapattayasuksa," which translates to "Architectural Education" in *Prachachat Newspaper*.[10] The author, who used the pseudonym Nai Sonchai, criticized the curriculum of the Faculty of Architecture at Chulalongkorn University for too closely following that of the School of Architecture at Liverpool University, thereby failing to adjust it to suit local Thai requirements. The author also claimed that the construction methods laid out in the textbooks could not be used in Siam as they would be too expensive, and that the breadth of the university's curriculum on Siamese architecture was too small. He was of the opinion that graduates were not being equipped with adequate practical knowledge and would, therefore, be put out of employment by experienced draughtspeople who have been working longer than these graduates, and who could probably do better than them, but with less salary.

5. To Be Progressive

Despite the many criticisms, the policy of the government in the development of architecture schools pursued its original

27

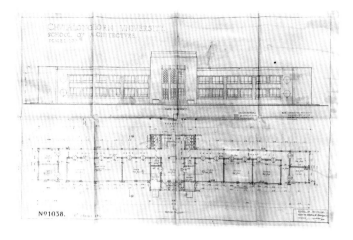

Figure 5
Ground-floor plan and front
elevation of Faculty of
Architecture building,
Chulalongkorn University,
1941

aim to train professional local architects that could substitute for European architects in the public sectors. On August 16, 1937, to develop the curriculum further, the government decided to employ a foreign professor as head of department, with a three-year contract.[11] Professor Lucien Coppé (1892–1975), a Belgian architect who had worked extensively in Bruges, took this position. Despite its aim to produce Siamese graduates to replace foreigners, the school could not help depending on yet another foreigner to make its plan come true. To assure the prestige of the department and the subjects taught, the curriculum of Chulalongkorn University's Faculty of Architecture needed a foreign professor believed to be able to help Siam strengthen this new subject and lift it to a high standard.

6. Modern cum Traditional: The Bachelor's Degree and the New Building

Despite the changes executed during Professor Coppé's tenure, Chulalongkorn University's Faculty of Architecture retained much of Liverpool University's School of Architecture's curriculum. The lessons still concentrated on Western classical orders and building types, and only English texts were used. However, the expectation of the People's Party government of the role of the university's Faculty of Architecture now was higher, involving a focus on both modernity and tradition.

Approaching World War II, the government came under the direction of nationalist, Prime Minister Plaek Phibunsongkhram, who also served as the rector of Chulalongkorn University. The intention of the government to train Thais to take over construction jobs from foreigners remained; it aimed to claim positions in not only the public sector, but also the private, which was also

Figure 6
Reliefs on the Faculty of
Architecture building,
Chulalongkorn University,
1941

Figure 7
Modern Thai ornament on capitals and windows of the Faculty of Architecture building, Chulalongkorn University, 1941

dominated by the Chinese, who were thought to work without "theory." In line with the government's aim to use architecture as a tool to "civilize" the country at the time of nation-building, the Faculty of Architecture aimed to train professionals who would be responsible for enabling this task. Adding to these goals was also a new one—for the government and Chulalongkorn University to revive Thai art and architecture to strengthen nationalism and reassure Thailand's place in the world of civilized nations. Thailand would be modern, yet history- and identity-rich.

In 1941, the faculty, for the first time after changing the curriculum to a bachelor's degree course, awarded bachelor degrees in architecture to five graduates. It moved into its first permanent building designed by Professor Coppé in the same year (Figure 4, page 27 and Figure 5, page 28). The building presented as a good manifesto for the school's ethos regarding an "appropriate" architecture of Thailand at the time.

Despite being symmetrical in plan, with its main porch and columns at the center (following Beaux-Arts principles), the building also revealed Coppé's experimentation, along the lines of modernism adapted to suit the local context. Parapets and reinforced-concrete eaves were used to respectively hide asbestos cement sheet roofing and shade the windows. Large glass windows were applied for classrooms and studios, making the most of natural light, while round windows lit stairs at both ends of the building. Between the large windows, Coppé placed a variety of geometric and abstract reliefs not seen in his previous works in Belgium or any other building in Thailand (Figure 6, page 28).[12] Adapted Thai ornaments were also applied for capitals and the decoration of front doors (Figure 7).

The description of these reliefs and capitals in the announcement of the building's opening ceremony reads: "Every column of the front façade has a particular pattern designed following architectural art. Especially at the entrance, Thai ornaments are used, such as for the capitals."[13]

At the end of 1941, during World War II, Thailand was forced into an alliance with Japan. During the war, shortages of drawing tools, paper, and pigment affected teaching.[14] Foreign magazines also became more difficult to acquire from bookshops. However, with regards to the aim of the government and the Faculty to "help Thais to research on existing Thai art, to give a good example, and to integrate it with modern knowledge in order to create architecture that particularly belongs to Thailand, that will be the everlasting culture of the nation," it was timely that the first text book, *Architecture in Thailand*, written in Thai by Nat Phothiprasat was published in 1944, to be used in the university and sold to the public.

7. Post-war Progress, Localization, and Modernism

In the postwar period, the number of architectural and engineering graduates were reported as being inadequate for the requirements of Thailand's government offices. Housing shortages, renovation projects for government buildings, and policies to improve rural dwelling conditions further accelerated the need for trained architects and engineers. However, even these situations still did not result in architecture being fully recognized by the public in the way that architects wished. Practical aspects and issues in the building process were paid more attention to than the aesthetics of the constructions.

Going back to the comment by Kridakorn in 1934 that the construction industry in the country needed to be developed alongside architectural practice and education, we could say that the industry after the war was relatively more developed than what it was in the 1930s. There were more Thai builders and contractors in the industry now, even some with good craftsmanship skills that were comparable to that of the Chinese. However, there were new challenges.

Following the war, material prices and wages increased dramatically, causing problems for both state and private construction projects. Mom Chao Vodhyakara Varavarn, as the new head of the Department of Architecture in the Faculty of Architecture at Chulalongkorn University in 1950 proposed a plan of research into alternative materials, sending students and lecturers abroad to learn new technologies for the improvement of the domestic situation.[15]

These plans revealed a typical idea of the relationship between imports and the locality regarding the transplantation of "Western" ideas and practices to Thailand. A relationship could be seen between M. C. Vodhyakara's call for research on local materials and his plan to send lecturers and students abroad to learn "new" technologies. The former action reiterated that conventional materials and construction methods mainly derived from the West needed to be adapted to the local context. Alternatives had to be studied and produced to substitute for the imported or mainstream domestic products that dominated the market, yet which were too expensive. The latter move, however, insisted on the necessity to import more radical new ideas, and possibly new technologies. These dual actions were seen as necessary as long as the stage of development in Thailand failed to reach the same standard as that in more developed countries.

Almost two decades after the establishment of modern architectural practice and schools in Thailand, where the transplantation of the concept, ideas, principles, and practice of architecture from the Western world to Thailand had been done mainly by means of "import," and research on an alternative, the new head of the department was calling for something to emerge locally. It might be considered ironic if we assume that this idea of M. C. Vodhyakara's stemmed from his Arts and Crafts background inspired by his teacher Edward Prior at Cambridge University, United Kingdom, which encouraged his creative use of local materials and vernacular architecture—which is in itself an imported idea. However, the way he understood the essence of such Western ideas seemed "appropriate" for the local conditions. The nineteenth-century Arts and Crafts's ideology of locality, different from the more universal Beaux-Arts concepts from Liverpool University, fitted itself to the practical aspect of an overseas case. At the same time, the quest for new imports was not neglected but encouraged. The postwar ambition and action of the leading Thai architect, reflected in the local education curriculum, remained a hybrid.

In 1951, the Faculty of Architecture had twenty-eight first year students, three of whom were women.[16] By requesting increased budgets, it aimed to admit fifty new students in 1953.[17] The material research initiated by M. C. Vodhyakara started with research on houses for farmers all over Thailand, as well as the construction of a prototype house, both of which were conducted between 1951 and 1952.

Urban Planning or Civic Architecture, a Liverpool University derivation, was previously taught only in the fifth year, but for the first time, was now included in the third-year year, but for the first time, was now included in the third-year

curriculum of the Faculty of Architecture.[18] A plan to establish a Department of Urban Planning in the Faculty of Architecture was also underway as the Act of Urban Planning had been issued and, therefore, the government needed people to work in this field.[19] A plan to establish a Department of Fine Arts was also initiated as the developing industry in the country needed to be value-added with art.[20]

In Europe, the postwar period saw radical changes in international architectural practice and education. Classical subjects were reduced and limited to the first half of the first year at Liverpool University.[21] By the mid-1950s, the Beaux-Arts method had been nearly excluded from architectural education in the United Kingdom.[22] While the curriculum at Liverpool University—the mold from which the curriculum for Chulalongkorn University was formed—started to move away from classics toward modernism; the curriculum of Chulalongkorn University remained largely unchanged until 1954.

An Nimmanhemin, a new teacher who was a fresh graduate of Liverpool University and Harvard University, United States, actually attempted to introduce modernist principles in the fourth year studio as early as 1950.[23] He recalled that the subject History still focused on classic, Gothic, Renaissance, and Thai architecture. Urban Planning or Civic Design focused on the study of ancient cities with exercises on garden design, but with a lack of economic, social, and administrative issues; Theory of Design also focused on classical principles. Students' works, therefore, showed classical influences, exploiting axes, symmetry, solidity, and massiveness. The understanding of construction, especially with reinforced concrete or wood was not shown much. Visits to the university by Richard Joseph Neutra (1952) and Walter Gropius (1953), who were received by professors, a few practitioners, and some students, seemed to have made little impact, but may have, at the very least, ignited an atmosphere of change.

However, in 1954, a seed of change was planted. M. C. Vodhyakara became the dean of the Faculty, and Nat Phothiprasat, who had been transferred to lead the government's Department of Municipal Works shortly after the establishment of the Department of Architecture in 1933, returned to be a full-time staff member. During his time at the Department of Municipal Works, his work had mainly demonstrated a geometric, cubic, and simple use of forms, as well as functional planning and the use of local materials, all of which had also been reflected in his writings and part-time-teaching from the beginning. He promoted "appropriateness"—that is rationality and economy—as a rationale behind his works.

If rationality was a main principle of modernism, then it was never far away from being the main principle of Thailand's first architecture school's ethos, right from its establishment. However, the distinction was that it had originated in the rationality of Beaux-Arts, and this was about to be linked with modernist rationality without a clear break. In practice, Western rationality, like other imported ideas gleaned from the analysis of foreign architecture books and magazines, had already been indigenized for the school. An example is highlighted M. C. Vodhyakara's welcome address to new students in 1952, in which he had stressed to students about using rationality over the personal fondness of forms:
"The Architect has a career like that of a god—he creates, not destroys, as Satan does. From my memory appears Phra Witsanukam, the god of construction. In every work of an architect, he deems to convey delight, mental pleasure, and visual pleasure

to people for his wisdom and that [wisdom] of fellow architects. Such wisdom would be achieved by an analysis of pure thinking being accompanied with rationality beyond the normal; beyond selfishness. The practice of pure thinking tends to be obstructed by a devil called Rakha who would distract the mind to slip away and mislead it toward a fondness for form. If this devil's power immerses itself into one's spirit, one's thinking can never be pure and rational and one cannot think beyond the normal. Therefore, it would be difficult for a person to elevate his creativity because his mind has been committed to the form about which he was passionate. The consequence is that he would just create a form. […] The wisdom that we look for is an infinite wisdom. It is permanent […] such as a paragon, bringing excellent architecture that remains great for hundreds of years; melodious music that will never be boring. […] Architects and artists from all eras, therefore, continuously practice the infinite wisdom. This is not unlike the religious way: practicing infinite wisdom—the way to nirvana."[24]

M. C. Vodhyakara was critical of the issue of rationality as he stated that students in their early years tended to be copyists, copying what they liked from magazines.[25] Therefore, he insisted that despite the course being similar to those in the United Kingdom and France, the differences in climate, living conditions, and available materials were crucial.[26] Another crucial and unresolved issue—which M. C. Vodhyakara claimed was not happening in Europe—was determining the appropriate "character" for modern Thai architecture, which he thought the school should set as a problem for students in the advanced years of their course.[27]

Amid the wind of change in international architecture education, the school finally reformed its curriculum toward modernism in 1954,

again following the curriculum of Liverpool University, which had turned its interest to Bauhaus designs. As a result, the subject of classical architecture was reduced significantly.

With regards to modernist influence from outside the classroom, architects' works and their articles in the *Association of Siamese Architects' Journal*, now republished as *ASA*, shows that modernist ideas were not explicit at the beginning of the 1950s. Toward the end of the decade, more accounts about what had been going on in the United States appeared in the journal, but they were at first superficial, gradually becoming more critical. This happened alongside the gradual appearance of a modernist grain in designs outside the classrooms. One of the pioneering examples of this was the World Travel Service office building, which was designed by the then dean of the Faculty of Architecture at Chulalongkorn University, M. C. Vodhyakara, which was completed in 1957 (Figure 8).

8. The School of Thai Architecture: A Modern Tradition?

For more than two decades, the Faculty of Architecture at Chulalongkorn University was the only higher learning architecture school in the country until a second one was established at Silpakorn University (also known as The University of Fine Arts of Thailand) in 1955. Amid the more conservative political circumstances that were generated under the second term of Prime Minister Plaek Phibunsongkhram—who now promoted national culture and art even more intensely to resist communism—the second school initially instructed on traditional Thai architecture. Thai art and architecture, treated as minor subjects at Chulalongkorn University, became the main part of the curriculum at the new school. While changing ideas in architectural practice, and Chulalongkorn University gradually moved toward modernism, the architecture course taught at Silpakorn University represented an achievement for the practice of traditional architecture that had long sought a way to incorporate Thai art into the contemporary architecture of the country. The overarching approach toward architecture at Silpakorn University was to mix Thai style with modern functions and apply Thai ornaments using modern materials such as concrete. However, even such noble notions, could not escape the changing situation in real life. Soon after its establishment, amid rapid economic development under a new generation of military dictators after 1957—which entailed a greater need for modern buildings and architects who could design them efficiently—the architecture school at Silpakorn University finally extended its curriculum to modern architecture in 1966, reducing Thai architecture again to the status of a minor subject.

9. Conclusion

More than two decades after its establishment, Chulalongkorn University struggled through shortages of staff and funding and deprivations created by World War II. Architecture training, like the practice of it, had to fight for its place in Thai society, since it was a new subject about which the public had no clear idea of, or even none at all. Pioneering teachers attempted to make sense of the subject for the students, most of whom also had had little idea about architecture. The process involved a localization of knowledge and ideas gained from advanced nations where the subject of architecture had already been established and had public interest, and an appreciation of art and architecture, in the Western sense—especially for their artistic value—was understood. As a result, Thai teachers faced the challenge of making sense of artistic value in architecture for students who would graduate to work in a society in which a necessity of functional and hygienic buildings was prioritized, and in most cases considered "enough." Further, these artistic values in architecture were based on the conventional principle of architecture learnt by Thai teachers in the West, but which started to be challenged by modernism soon after these pioneers left school. Before they could establish such values in their students' minds and in their own country, the situation again started to change. They, therefore, had to catch up with new ideas, knowledge and technology, only to localize them and adapt them to suit the local context again. This was because it was not fully relevant to apply modernist values or machine aesthetics in a country where an industrial revolution had never taken place, and where the livelihood of the majority remained mostly unchanged. The teachers, therefore, tended to merge the new ideas with old rationales that they had not yet fully established in the field and society. In this sense, the "rationality" of modernism did not differ significantly from the "rationailty" of classicism in the Thai context.

The attempt to search for a contemporary position for traditional art, as opposed to a wholesale import of the new, also faced difficulties: Where should the balance be placed, and how should it be done? The number of experts and resources was also limited. By the time the teachers successfully established an institution to teach such art, they realized that the society, which was still struggling with modernity, was not yet ready to support a revival—ironically, itself a modern concept.

Notes
1. Luang Sukkhawatthanasunthon, "Withi Damnoen Kan Kosang Saphan Phra Buddhayotfa Khong Borisat Dorman Long Phurapmao" ["Construction Methods of Phra Buddhayotfa Bridge by Dorman Long Company, Contractor"], *Khao Chang*, special issue (1932), 173–174.
2. Tiptus, *Sathapanik Siam: Puen Than Bot Bat Pon Ngan Lae Naew Kid (Po So 2475–2537) [Siamese Architects: Foundation, Roles, Works, and Concepts (AD 1932–1990)]*, 30.
3. National Archives of Thailand, S R 0201.14/2.
4. Andrew Saint, *Architect and Engineer: A Study in Sibling Rivalry* (New Haven, London: Yale University Press, 2008), 467.
5. Tiptus, *Sathapanik Siam: Puen Than Bot Bat Pon Ngan Lae Naew Kid*, 59.
6. *Ratchakitchanubaeksa [The Royal Thai Government Gazette]* vol 52 (1935): 82.
7. Tiptus, *Sathapanik Siam: Puen Than Bot Bat Pon Ngan Lae Naew Kid*, 50.
8. An interview with An Nimmanhemin, quoted from Tiptus, *Sathapanik Siam: Puen Than Bot Bat Pon Ngan Lae Naew Kid (Po So 2475–2537) [Siamese Architects: Foundation, Roles, Works, and Concepts (AD 1932–1990)]*, 60.
9. Kridakorn, *Rueng Kiaokab Sathapattayakam [About Architecture]*, 39.
10. Nai Son Chai, "Sathapattayasuksa" ["Architectural Education"], *Prachachat*, May 7, 1936. The government's Office of Advertisement sent the article to the Faculty of Architecture at Chulalongkorn University and it was kept in Chulalongkorn University Archives, Ch 10, Box 1, Folder 15, labeled "Khana Sathapattayakam" ["Faculty of Architecture"].
11. "Chulalongkorn University Employs Foreigners," National Archives of Thailand, Bangkok, Thailand, S R 0201.19/47.
12. An interview with Chaloem Rattanathatsani, Professor Lucien Coppé's assistant, as quoted in Tiptus, *Sathapanik Siam: Puen Than Bot Bat Pon Ngan Lae Naew Kid (Po So 2475–2537) [Siamese Architects: Foundation, Roles, Works, and Concepts (AD 1932–1990)]*, 729.
13. *Kan Poed Tuek Tangtang Nai Wanchat [The Opening of New Buildings on the National Day]*, 22. Chulalongkorn University Archives, Bangkok, Thailand, Ch 18.5, Box 1, Folder 5.
14. Tiptus, *Sathapanik Siam: Puen Than Bot Bat Pon Ngan Lae Naew Kid*, 29
15. "The Committee for Sourcing Construction Materials and Labour," National Archives of Thailand, Bangkok, Thailand (2) S R 0201.69/57.
16. "Khao Chak Rongrian Khao" ["News from the Old School"], *ASA 1* (1951): 51–58.
17. "The Improvement and Extension in Subjects of Chulalongkorn University," National Archives of Thailand, Bangkok, Thailand, (3) S R 0201.59.1/17.
18. "Khao Chak Rongrian Khao" ["News from the Old School"].
19. "Khrongkan Raya 5 Pi Khana Sathapattayakammasat Chulalongkorn Mahawitthayalai" ["A 5-Year Plan for the Faculty of Architecture, Chulalongkorn University"], 1951, M. C. Vodhyakara Varavarn's Archives, Bangkok, Thailand, 1951.
20. ibid, 1–2.
21. An Nimmanhaemin, "Khwam Plianplaeng Khrang Yingyai Nai Khana Sathapat Thi Khaphachao Dai Ru Haen Ma" ["The Great Change in the Faculty of Architecture That I Have Known"], *ASA 2* (1958): 22–27; Nimmanhaemin studied at Liverpool University at the time.
22. Mark Crinson and Jules Lubbock, *Architecture—Art or Profession?: Three Hundred Years of Architectural Education in Britain*, 5.
23. An Nimmanhaemin, "Khwam Plianplaeng Khrang Yingyai Nai Khana Sathapat Thi Khaphachao Dai Ru Haen Ma" ["The Great Change in the Faculty of Architecture That I Have Known"].
24. "Tonrab Nisit Mai" ["Welcoming New Students"], 1952, M. C. Vodhyakara Varavarn's Archives, Bangkok, Thailand.
25. M. C. Vodhyakara Varavarn's letter to Mr. Brown, 1952, M. C. Vodhyakara Varavarn's Archives, Bangkok, Thailand.
26. ibid.
27. ibid.

Figure Credits
Figure 1: A studio work of the Faculty of Architecture at Chulalongkorn University, created between 1939 and 1941 (*Pluk Ban Phid Kid Chon Ban Thalai [Building a House Wrongly, the Owner Will Be Upset Until it Collapses]*, printed as a memorial book for the funeral of Unchit Wasuwat and Phaichit Wasuwat (Bangkok, Thailand: Rong Phim Sri Krung, 1942)).
Figure 2: A work of Unchit Wasuwat, a student at Chulalongkorn University from 1939 to 1941, showing a composition of classical elements following Beaux-Arts principles (as Figure 1 above).
Figure 3: The measured works and reconstruction of an ancient monument showing Phra Prang Wat Phraram; by Unchit Wasuwat, a student at Chulalongkorn University from 1939 to 1941 (as Figure 1 above).
Figure 4: Faculty of Architecture building at Chulalongkorn University designed by Lucien Coppé, 1941 (Chulalongkorn University Archives, Bangkok, Thailand).
Figure 5: Ground-floor plan and front elevation of Faculty of Architecture building, Chulalongkorn University, 1941 (Chulalongkorn University Archives, Bangkok, Thailand).
Figure 6: Reliefs on the Faculty of Architecture building, Chulalongkorn University, 1941 (author's photo).
Figure 7: Modern Thai ornament on capitals and windows of the Faculty of Architecture building, Chulalongkorn University, 1941 (author's photo).
Figure 8: The World Travel Service office building, designed by M. C. Vodhyakara Varavarn and completed in 1957 reflects a modernist grain in its design (courtesy of Beer Singnoi).

Status-appropriate Spaces: How Bangkok's Architecture Negotiates Formal and Informal Thai Values

Philip **CORNWEL-SMITH**, Freelance Writer, Thailand; author of *Very Thai: Everyday Popular Culture* and *Very Bangkok: In the City of the Senses*

Abstract

Bangkok, Thailand, is typically considered an unplanned mess. Yet, through the lens of cultural values, it is possible to re-evaluate the architectural rationales and rival visions, rendering the city more coherent. This study examines local beliefs, ideologies, and cultural traits that have shaped the Thai capital's urban character. It analyses Bangkok's origins as a sacred embodiment of divine rule, through its reinvention as a *siwilai* (civilized) metropole that localized imported styles to its freewheeling growth as an industrial megalopolis. Cultural traits reveal how the city has handled migration, catered to an aspirational middle class, and overlaid modern infrastructure atop an ancient layout designed for a social cantonment. As urbanists try to make sense of Bangkok's unique built environment, conceptual frameworks tend to highlight the role of informal, often temporary, structures that planners and officials dismiss. This approach goes beyond traditional architectural history to address emergent movements like "messy urbanism," theories based on Thai social mores, and independent initiatives by landscape architects, to seek a fuller understanding of Thai urbanism.

Author Information
Philip CORNWEL-SMITH: philcornwelsmith@me.com

Keywords

Cultural values, Thai cities, planning, informal sector, messy urbanism, architectural history.

The urbanism of Bangkok, Thailand, presents a first (and enduring) impression of chaos, or at the very least, an organic urban organism that resists order. The Thai capital's buildings are a bewildering mix of styles—many hybrid—with few indigenous remnants. Yet, there are methods in Bangkok's apparent mess.

Often quoted as "unplanned," Bangkok is actually a battleground of rival plans, though none prevailing, due to corruption, poor enforcement, and competing interests. Sacredness continues to animate architecture in this cosmopolitan megalopolis, vying with differing visions of modernity and an eclectic taste for novelty. That ferment leaves freedom for jarring juxtapositions and a vast informal street life that resists the forces of order.

This look at the values behind Bangkok's built environment spotlights an architectural legacy of each trait. It draws upon my latest book, *Very Bangkok: In the City of the Senses*,[1] which explains from multiple perspectives why Bangkok is the way it is.

1. Thai-ness

Anyone involved in Thai arts, architects especially, can't escape being judged in terms of "Thai-ness." Periodically, cultural gatekeepers condemn buildings for the misuse of sacred Thai designs, like resorts that riff on temple forms. Such vehemence is a clue that Thai style is more about ideals than aesthetics.

Thai-ness is not a description of things found here, nor is it pure tradition. Thai-ness is an ideology for unifying the country's indigenous diversity into one national culture, under the "three pillars" of nation, religion, and monarchy. It instils conformity to Bangkokian norms, with templates for design, approved modes of dressing and manners, and even rules of what is Thai or un-Thai. Curiously, those rules keep changing.

This ideology began with Thai nationalism a century ago, then reversed between the 1932 Siamese revolution and the mid-1940s, during which a secular military dictatorship issued draconian cultural mandates that equated Thai-ness to tidiness, obedience, and modernity. These decreed most traditions and ethnic identities as "un-Thai," and regulated Thai-ness by instilling uniforms, discipline, and daily nationalist rituals. Those rules altered again after the 1976 coup with a neo-traditional revival, yet those cultural mandates remain key to understanding Thai policy, attitudes, and design.

1.1 Legacy: Icon Siam

The most prominent corporate showcase of Thai-ness is a giant riverside mall, Icon Siam (Figure 1). Thai arts, products, and imagery fill the complex, which has tiers of pleated glass modeled on a *krathong*, which is a basket made from folding a banana leaf to float a lamp during rituals or the Loy Krathong festival. The mall's indoor market, a cornucopia of food and crafts, is arranged according to Thailand's regions, with faux-provincial architecture. By hosting cultural spectacles, Icon Siam acts as a stage for the performance of Thai-ness.

2. Spires

Thailand's most distinctive architectural element is the roof. The ornate spired roofs of temples, shrines and palaces are conceived as the abode of deities, rather than of the humans who dwell below. These delicate shelters float above the humdrum. Like the

Figure 1
Icon Siam, 2018

Figure 2
Spirit house at the nightclub
Twisted, 2008

spire on a dancer's crown, they're disconnected from the ground and point heavenward. To Thais, the head is sacred and feet profane—a hierarchy that is extended to construction, as typically seen in the varied levels in a stilt house and in the stepped plinths on altars for ranking effigies of deities.

The basic unit of Thai architecture is the *sala*, which is a raised, open pavilion that is essentially a blank space under a pointy roof. The easiest way, therefore, to make a structure neo-traditional would be to add such a roof. The original model of this hybrid was the Chakri Maha Prasat Throne Hall in the Grand Palace on Bangkok's Rattanakosin Island. With three gilded spires atop a neo-Renaissance edifice, it was nicknamed "*farang* (Westerner) with a Thai hat," spelling out who's at the more "reverent" top.

2.1 Legacy: Contemporary Spirit Houses
Neo-traditional architecture may be a waning fashion for buildings, but it remains in vogue for designing the spirit house that must be present on each plot of Thai land, whether for residential, commercial or official use. Any improvement in the building also requires an upgrade to the spirit house, so that the land spirit doesn't cause trouble in the human abode. While most spirit houses have a generic temple look in painted masonry, modern designs are now common, often matching the building, but must have a sacred roof or spire and a precinct for the effigies and offerings. Often, architects, as a signature design statement, conjure futuristic, minimalist spirit houses in modern materials, like the all-glass one at the nightclub Twisted (Figure 2).

3. Mandala

If Bangkok's old town feels like a fantastical mirage, that's because its core buildings are a physical projection of mythology. Like many Indic cities, the original walled capital was conceived in 1782 as a sacred space and named Rattanakosin, which was later renamed with the auspicious title, Krungthep (City of Angels). Its layout was arranged to become a mandala—a sacred diagram of Hindu-Buddhist cosmology—overlaid upon the moated Rattanakosin island it's said, it was shaped to evoke a Brahmin conch shell.

The capital had briefly been Thonburi (1767–82) after the destruction of the preceding capital of Ayutthaya by the Burmese. Krungthep was then conceived as a symbolic restoration of Ayutthaya, with temples and palaces replicated at set positions. Ayutthaya had itself been based upon Ayodhya, the Indian city of Prince Rama, an avatar of Vishnu and the hero of the Indian epic, *Ramayana*. The Thai version, *Ramakien*, still guides traditional design. Old Bangkok is a recreation of a recreation of a myth.

A mandala is typically centered upon Meru, the mountain of the gods. Symbolically, everyone has their place in this cosmological landscape, with karma dictating how far that spot is from the power center, and on which level on the steep central mount. Bangkok's icon, the temple Wat Arun, expresses this mandala in its elegantly distended *prang* (spires). Even Bangkok's gold-topped condominium Jambu Dvipa is themed on the continent of humans in the Meru mandala.

3.1 Legacy: Sappaya-Sapasathan Parliament House
Mandalic cosmology might seem arcane, but is a mental map that has been scaled up to even state level. Thai

Figure 3
Sappaya-Sapasathan
Parliament House, 2021

society is now less rigid, but one's status in life is based on this vertical hierarchy, while the distance from the center, also affects life profoundly.

The now-demolished old Parliament House, designed in Brasilia-style brutalism in 1974, had open horizontal lines with an egalitarian ethos. Its replacement, Sappaya-Sapasathan (Figure 3), is the world's biggest parliament building. An opaque mountain of glass and stone, it evokes Meru and the Buddhist monument of Borobudur in Java, Indonesia.

The winning design by Teerapol Niyom is audaciously a mandala, complete with sun and moon halls for members of parliament and senators respectively. The concept aligns with traditionalists' goals of a "Thai-style democracy" that draws its legitimacy less from the electorate and more from the top-down, under Buddhistic Thai-ness.

4. Siwilai

The pride Thailand carries from having avoided colonization by European nations still motivates how Thais present their capital. Imperialists had used a Christian civilizing mission to justify taking lands they considered primitive. Siam (renamed Thailand in 1939) pre-empted that "ploy" by adopting Western architecture, clothing, technology, and manners via strategic policies and elite tastes, so as to be *siwilai* (civilized).

One *siwilai* strategy was to shift the court around the turn of the twentieth century from Rattanakosin to Dusit, a suburb on a European grid with tree-lined avenues off Ratchadamnoen Road, which was a boulevard based on the Avenue des Champs-Élysée of Paris, France. Italian

architects were hired to erect palaces, ministries, and public buildings in neo-classical, Venetian Byzantine, art nouveau or Lombard liberty styles.

The plan was to instil shame upon indigenous and provincial cultures for being less *siwilai* than the imposed national culture, which is a hybrid of the central plains culture with imported elements. This multi-tier attitude privileges official Thai-ness and the elite's international tastes over indigenous folk ways, ethnic subcultures, and urban popular culture.

Siwilai tastes still steer development. Malls and planners often move messy street stalls into tidy aisles indoors. Corporations operate private compounds like the malls Asiatique and Yodpiman River Walk (Bangkok), which look like market lanes but are in fact gated "pseudo public spaces." The government's Rattanakosin Island Plan is less about conservation than it is about placemaking. It showcases the prestige of landmarks by removing nearby structures, no matter how historic, to emulate European-style open vistas that are picturesque, but alien to Bangkok's dense, eclectic urbanism.

4.1 Legacy: Queen Sirikit National Convention Centre

Thailand has long promoted a *siwilai* face to global powers by erecting showpiece halls. For a World Bank meeting in 1991, the Queen Sirikit National Convention Centre (QSNCC) in Bangkok (Figure 4, page 37) trumpeted Thai-style modernity by brandishing distilled shapes from Siamese architecture; dignitaries of the 2003 APEC Summit encountered neoclassical pastiche at the Royal Thai Navy Convention Hall (Bangkok). For the 2022 APEC summit, QSNCC was rebuilt five times its original size by the same architect, Design 103 International, with subtler accents that reference the elegant use of Thai crafts in tribute to the sponsorship of crafts by Queen Sirikit, the Queen Mother. Softening the scale, QSNCC's 200-meter-long curved curtain glazing opens onto Bangkok's biggest park and illuminates the textile-inspired "storytelling" décor by Onion.

5. Horizontal to Vertical City

Since 2000, Bangkok has pivoted from a horizontal network of villages into a vertical metropolis. In the preceding few decades, citizens who were used to being hemmed behind walls had sprawled across a vast floodplain with no natural limits, and housing estates replaced paddy fields and plantations. Travel writer Paul Theroux had even dubbed the city a "flattened anthill."

Having consumed the delta, Bangkok today now eats itself. When the city had reached commuting limits, developers filled in the gaps. Denser towers were built upon garden compounds that became noticeable from the BTS Skytrain, one of Bangkok's mass transit rail services. Shophouses had made most areas look alike, but an ever-morphing skyline of distinctive towers started to become reference points for one's location. Vertical living in Bangkok is marketed through condominium developments like Vertic, Vertiq, and The Vertical. Going vertical reveals many social inequalities, with height relating to seniority. Around the many towers of the affluent, most Bangkokians live in small houses or tiny studios in generic blocks that can't be adapted, whereas for centuries before, traditional Thai wooden housing had always been prefabricated, modular, and adjustable.

Above the messy, lower-status street life, sky bridges increasingly connect offices to condos and malls to stations with *siwilai* landscaped walkways. The elevated concourse at EmQuartier (a mall) evokes New York's High Line, an elevated linear park in the US.

5.1 Legacy: Mahanakhon

Bangkok's tallest tower from 2016–19, King Power Mahanakhon (formerly MahaNakhon), has a unique "eroded" design (Figure 5, page 38). German architect Ole Scheeren, who was consulted on this project—and who also designed Beijing's two-legged CCTV tower—was inspired by his time in 1998 co-curating the Bangkok iteration of the roving international art project "Cities on the Move." The tower's design embodies the part-built, part-decayed character of the cityscape. The gigantic tower cuboid is indented with a "disintegrating" spiral of pixellated boxes, which Thais compare to a 314-meter-high game of Jenga. From the Mahanakhon tower, hierarchical Bangkok looks down at its past and up at its future.

6. Enclaves

Walls defined the old Bangkok, segregating its subcultures into enclaves. The king used to live in a walled palace within a walled inner court, within the walled mini city of the Grand Palace, within the walled city of Rattanakosin. Skirting that royal citadel walls further enclosed a city of noble mansions. And outside these walls, minority groups were confined to their small quarters.

There wasn't just one Chinatown, or one quarter each for Mon, Muslims, Lao or Portuguese and so on. Each ethnic group and subgroup had multiple quarters, which were were located on the domains of whichever patron brought them to Bangkok. Some were

Figure 4
Queen Sirikit National
Convention Centre
(QSNCC), 2022

Figure 5
King Power Mahanakhon,
2016

in the entourage of the King, who directly ran southern Bangkok. Others arrived under the Viceroy (a rank abolished in 1885), who ran northern Bangkok. Further, groups were settled by branches of the influential Bunnag clan on their estates on the west bank of the river. Earlier ethnic settlements had dated from the Thonburi and Ayutthaya eras. This diverse ethnic patchwork remains a source of identity and charm, albeit being an eroding one.

Bangkok's urban model is a scaled-up village, which happens to be a parochiality that still hampers planning and development. Mega blocks of crowded, dead-end lanes with few access points are skirted by highways, explaining Bangkok's lack of secondary routes and through-roads.

This enclave pattern has become a habit, replicated first in walled family compounds, later in countless gated *moo baan* (housing estates), and now in the defensive architecture that separates patrolled condominium perimeters from common folk. Physical walls—and walls in the mind—have given Bangkok an atomized character it's never lost.

6.1 Legacy: Baan Baan

Kudi Jeen is one of Bangkok's best known, and longest existing, multi-ethnic enclaves, while the Leuenrit Community in Chinatown is a recent restoration of an intact traditional enclave. This typology of the urban village influences a *moo baan* housing estate that has been reimagined in retro style at Viphavadee Soi 20 in northern Bangkok known as Baan Baan—a phrase that means homely, rustic or villagey; it features design accents from traditional houses and markets.

Figure 6
Yossapon Boonsom of Shma
Co., Ltd, 2019

7. Background City

Bangkok operates on two grids that overlap but barely interact: a modern, high-status foreground grid that is superimposed upon an ancient, low-status background grid that grew organically from ethnic enclaves, informal settlements, and a waterborne culture. To see the hidden network, the visualizing tool Depth Map embodies data in ways that reveal the hidden network, such as a planned foreground of rail, roads, malls, and landmarks in warm tones, with a blue underlay of capillary lanes and community hubs, achieved by adjusting the program's filters. Most other maps, even the ones online, tend to miss this granular detail of local gathering spots and nodes for "background transit," like canal boats, *songtaew* pickup buses, and motorcycle taxis. Depth Map reveals Bangkok's hidden human-scale layers.

However, the mindset of today's planners has yet to conceive linking old transit with new, for that would mean mingling low with high status people. BTS Skytrain started service as an elevated domain priced beyond the masses. Its lines passed, but didn't link to two provincial bus stations, one of which was immediately moved. However, this is slowly changing with more intersections of formal and informal layers.

7.1 Legacy: Talad Phlu MRT Station

It was intended that the skytrain station at Saphan Taksin would be closed when the line crossed the river, however, it has had to remain open as it ended up linking to the express boat network, a background transit that has become mainstream. Now, more stations interlink with river and canal piers, like Sanam Chai MRT Station beside the rebuilt Ratchinee Pier. At the gigantic Talat Phlu MRT Station, seven layers of transit overlap, with two rail lines and concourse atop a flyover, a footbridge, the road, and a canal lined by temples and teetering wooden houses. The challenge and opportunity for architects is to construct ways to unite the foreground and background grids.

8. Squeezeways

Beyond Bangkok's spacious compounds, everything else gets crammed into the disorderly spaces in between. The city jams nine million vehicles onto roads designed only for 1.5 million, that cover just eight per cent of the built-up area, which is about half the ideal surface and a third that of Paris. In his novel of a dystopian future Bangkok, *The Windup Girl*,[2] Paolo Bacigalupi called these narrow routes "squeezeways."

Thanon (roads) are fed by *soi* (lanes, or literally dividers), branching into *trok* (alleys) and *sork* (dead-end "elbow" spurs), often without sidewalks. The *soi* originated as the irrigation ditches bordering rice fields and plantations, hence the many ninety-degree turns within them. In the absence of plazas, *soi* and *sork* became a space to shop, work and play. Similarly, *pak soi* ("mouths" where lanes meet roads) are likened to the way floating markets formerly arose at canal confluences, abuzz with petty traders as vehicles and people slipped through the tumult. This pattern recurs, with housing estates accessed via maze-like *sois*. This always constant proximity, together with jutting sunshades render Bangkok as a close-up city of glimpsed partial views, not panoramas.

8.1 Legacy: Bangrak and Khlong San Creative District

Under-appreciated by planners, the dense background grid of lanes and shophouses are becoming recognized as the connective tissue of Bangkok's urban culture, and its crafts and markets as the taproots of Thai creativity. In recent years, a group made up of landscape architects, community representatives, local traders, and incoming startups has acted as an independent planner in founding a creative district along two neglected but gentrifying riverside districts, Bangrak and Khlong San. The relocation of the Thailand Creative & Design Center to the Grand Postal Building provided the creative district with a physical focus, from which a new route to the River City art mall area was opened via a private path through Warehouse 30, a hub of galleries, cafés, and boutiques.

Its support of indigenous urbanism is exemplified by Yossapon Boonsom of the landscape architecture firm Shma Co., Ltd (Figure 6, page 38), whose social enterprise arm creates community amenities and green space through the WePark project. Another founder and activist, architect Duangrit Bunnag, asserted in his "Bangkok Manifesto" at the BangkokEdge ideas festival in 2016: "Trying to portray the city as a problem is the real problem."

9. Impromptu Architecture

Bangkok is famed for its hectic street life, which prizes practicality before aesthetics. The city's huge informal sector was not respected as part of Thai-ness when my book about it, *Very Thai: Everyday Popular Culture*,[3] came out in 2005. Informal urbanism has since come to be treated more as culture, though it is under labels such as "*thai thai*" (Thai-ish), "*baan baan*" (rustic) or "very Thai."

When Bangkok was lauded by CNN for having the world's best street food, officials shocked many by purging street food from most areas to "reclaim public space." They did allow promotional street food zones for tourists, ignoring its prime function as affordable mass nutrition. It was a spasm of shame, that the city's "face" was being usurped by messy, low-status trade that was not under any official control.

Street food was only in the street because it began as migrant food cooked for migrants without kitchens at home. Most of it derives from China, India, or northeast Thailand. Besides, Thais demand convenience, hence the plethora of stalls and traders lining Bangkok's squeezeways. Ever more venues bring street food into indoor settings, often styled like old wooden markets; but at stake is also the city's communal character.

Lately, a radical rethink of developing cities has spawned the concept of "messy urbanism," which sets aside perfectionism to upgrade through informal mechanisms like village organization, itinerant vending, or handmade transit; "messy urbanism" is inconceivable to the tidy-minded. Said the bureaucrat who purged those markets in emulation of Singapore: "The city [hall] could not equate the charm of Bangkok with untidiness."

Regardless, the growing Thai movement against the seniority system overlaps with creatives who champion the informal sector's ingenuity. In media and exhibitions, vendor carts get deconstructed as exemplar Thai temporary mobile structures. Whole restaurants get folded into a box on wheels, hooked to a motorbike, and then unfolded at a new site under umbrellas and awnings. Young architect Chatchawan Suwansawat is known for his technical sketches of "everyday architecture," from trolleys and racks to parking barriers and devices improvized from scrap materials.

39

Figure 7
Chang Chui, 2017

9.1 Legacy: Chang Chui

As mega projects replace whole blocks, Bangkok loses its human scale, diversity and types of distinctly Thai informal spaces. Architects like CHAT Architects, with their "Bangkok Bastards" initiative, are seeking ways to develop whilst retaining the animated street life and community vibe. A Thai fashion designer, Somchai Songwattana of Fly Now, a Thai fashion brand, founded a multi-use complex of ad hoc buildings with an adaptive style that hosts markets and festivals that channel the spirit of Thai messy urbanism. The name of this place, Chang Chui (Figure 7), means "untidy artisan."

10. Kalatesa

The notion of cultural rules feels counterintuitive in a place so seemingly casual and inconsistent. It all depends on which rules, when, where, and for whom. Thais broadly observe customs and taboos, whereas laws and regulations carry less respect, or rather, are often seen to favor those with influence.

Navigating the ambiguity is done through the unwritten codes of *kalatesa* (time—space), so Thais are constantly on the alert, ready to adapt to the situation, status relations, and what's deemed "appropriate." One implicit rule is that rules don't apply to those with impunity. In Thai architecture, demarcations of height and space express seniority and are most visible in palaces and temples.

10.1 Legacy: Wat Pariwat

Beliefs, conventions and templates determine the design of sacred spaces. Yet as long as *kalatesa* is observed, there is huge leeway to innovate or amuse. Amid all the *lai thai* (traditional patterns), another visible Thai trait is the appropriation of modern imports. The new Wat Pariwat temple in Bangkok (Figure 8, page 41) shows how playfulness can enliven a rigid structure. Inside and out, it's coated with sculptural characters of eclectic origins. A gilded David Beckham statue peeks out from the plinth of a Buddha image, while cowboys, samurai, and even Shakespeare all loom out of the mosaic reliefs. You can also read the positions of pop culture's representatives in the hierarchy, with Pikachu and Popeye positioned low down, Einstein and Batman on the walls, and Chinese literary characters atop the roof.

11. *Lak-ka-pid Lak-ka-perd*

The Thai affinity for adaptive structures depends on timing and social context. According to writer Sopawan Boonnimitra, "[kalatesa] still prevails, particularly the way in which space is quite fragmented and there are no clear boundaries, as can still be seen in Thai mural paintings." In her thesis of the same name,[4] she labels this spatial ambiguity *lak-ka-pid lak-ka-perd* (sometimes shut, sometimes open), a "social chameleon" reference that came about in reference to gender minorities, but which just as easily suits the adjustment to appropriateness.

The paucity of public spaces leads to their periodic temporary use by *talad nat* (appointment markets), at intervals that could be annual, seasonal, monthly, weekly, or in shifts throughout the day. Such switching enables multipurpose sites to phase vendors, making efficient time-based use of limited space.

The archetype of this format—temple fairs—have overlapping periods of being sacred, *sanuk* (fun), cultural, and commercial.

Figure 8
Wat Pariwat, 2019

Thai monasteries have always had a multifunction community ground that could alternately or simultaneously be used for education, healing, vending, eating, or entertainment. As this format appeals deeply to the ways and practices of Thai people, newer developments—such as mall forecourts or institutions like Museum Siam or Bangkok Art & Culture Centre (BACC)—are designed to host a variety of temporary occasions.

11.1 Legacy: Bangkok Design Week
Many contemporary events such as youth festivals, Lit Fest, or Bangkok Edge utilize the fair format with multiple kinds of activity held in spaces easily adapted to host art, music, dining, exhibitions, entertainment, games, stalls, or campaigns.

Thailand Creative and Design Center (TCDC) holds many of Bangkok Design Week's installations in old communities, shrines, and social venues, as well as "surprise" buildings each year. Festivals like Ghost, Art in Soi, and Bangkok Art Biennale, likewise, hold shows in locations that range from previously inaccessible landmarks to forgotten architectural sites that are slated to be demolished or converted, like Bumrung Nukulkit Printing House (Figure 9, page 42). This selecting of unusual spaces for a short time period chimes with the impermanent nature of Bangkok and helps citizens appreciate their urban inheritance.

12. Impermanent Heritage

Bangkok is a palimpsest—a city of layers in which you can read those social values from fossils in the architectural strata. The past isn't fully wiped away, yet what remains is often not well maintained and gets augmented with ad-hoc insertions. The integrity of its streetscapes depends on Thai attitudes to old buildings: what's kept, what's altered, and what's erased.

The restoration of heritage hinges on local values that favor change over continuity. The corrosive monsoon climate breeds a tendency for replacement over repair, using modern materials for an "as-new" look, removing the patina of age that here is only a niche taste. Buddhism emphasizes the present over the past or future, while a belief from Hindu origin holds that sacred structures must be intact to embody the divine. Crucially, a "face culture" is motivated to keep things up-to-date, and to regard what's old as having lower status—unless converting an old building gains the owner "face."

What's considered heritage in Bangkok isn't just age, rarity, or importance, but more so whether it qualifies under Thai-ness. Architectural treasures are vulnerable if they lack links to national culture—such as the patrimony of commoners and minorities. Bangkok's urban and commercial architecture is inseparable from its Sino-Thai settlers. Chinatown's thousands of heritage-worthy structures are gazetted, though officially, still unprotected. Often, buildings are the last trace of subcultures that the state ignores or erases.

Mid-twentieth-century modernism has recently gained some recognition, though just as the best examples of hotels, cinemas, and brutalist concrete were pulled down. It's not just because they're less old; modernism in Thailand is inseparable from the political and cultural "fresh-start" initiated by the 1932 Siamese revolution. Since the violent coup of 1976, ultra-conservatives have sought to erase that 1932 legacy and promote neo-traditional arts and architecture. A new Thai-roofed Supreme Court replaced the original modernist court, which was erected to institute the constitutional rule of law. However, today's anti-establishment

Figure 9
Bumrung Nukulkit Printing
House (established 1895) at
Bangkok Design Week 2021

protest movement overlaps with fresh interest in modernism. In Bangkok, architectural taste can reveal a political stance.

Conserving a Bangkok building largely remains a private initiative that requires delicate negotiation. Ultimately, deference to influential people makes preservation hard to achieve and enforce. An abbot of Wat Kalayanamit (Bangkok) razed many registered monuments. Every Thai preservation body—public, professional, and official—campaigned to save the Scala Cinema (the last standalone single-screen cinema in Bangkok) and Bangkok's last early Rattanakosin-era wooden houses at Pom Mahakan, yet their destruction could not be stopped.

Bangkok's architecture is in constant churn. For decades, developers have been fitting major buildings within the patchwork streetscape, typified by the irregular footprints of Emporium and Terminal 21 malls. In a dramatic recent shift, architectural diversity is being lost as mega projects replace entire city blocks. Bangkokians simply shrug.

Thai culture has always had temporary structures, from market stalls to moveable wooden houses pegged from modular panels and poles. Buddhism teaches that clinging on to anything breeds dissatisfaction, and this Theravada-majority metropolis embraces that impermanence, to build, or rebuild, in the moment.

Notes
1. Philip Cornwel-Smith, *Very Bangkok: In the City of the Senses* (London/Bangkok: River Books, 2020).
2. Paolo Bacigalupi, *The Windup Girl* (United States: Night Shade Books, 2009).
3. Philip Cornwel-Smith, *Very Thai: Everyday Popular Culture* (London/Bangkok: River Books, 2004; Second edition, 2013).
4. Sopawan Boonnimitra, "*Lak-ka-pid lak-ka-perd*," [thesis], Lunds Universitet, Sweden, 2006.

Figure Credits
Figure 1: Icon Siam, 2018 (author's photo).
Figure 2: Spirit house at the nightclub Twisted, 2008 (author's photo).
Figure 3: Sappaya-Sapasathan Parliament House, 2021 (author's photo).
Figure 4: Queen Sirikit National Convention Centre (QSNCC), 2022 (author's photo).
Figure 5: King Power Mahanakhon, 2016 (author's photo).
Figure 6: Yossapon Boonsom of Shma Co., Ltd, 2019 (author's photo).
Figure 7: Chang Chui, 2017 (author's photo).
Figure 8: Wat Pariwat, 2019 (author's photo).
Figure 9: Bumrung Nukulkit Printing House (established 1895) at Bangkok Design Week 2021 (author's photo).

Architecture Asia and the Pursuit of Discourse on Contemporary Asian Architecture—Record of "Thailand Contemporary Architecture Forum"

ZHOU Minghao, Managing Editor, *Architecture Asia*; Associate Professor, College of Architecture and Urban Planning, Tongji University
***WANG Yanze**, Executive Editor, *Architecture Asia*; Assistant Professor, College of Architecture and Urban Planning, Tongji University
ZHENG Xin, Assistant Editor, *Architecture Asia*

Author Information
ZHOU Minghao: zhouminghao@tongji.edu.cn
WANG Yanze (*corresponding author): wangyanze029@hotmail.com
ZHENG Xin: xin.zheng.10@outlook.com

Abstract

Architecture Asia is the official journal of the Architects Regional Council Asia (ARCASIA). Since 2020, when the Architectural Society of China (ASC) and Tongji University undertook the editing work as the journal's co-publishers, the journal has been dedicated to transforming from a traditional printed publication to a new media platform. The Tongji editorial team has built an eco-chain of "project display + academic discussion" through various approaches, including publications and forums, to reveal contemporary architectural developments in Asia. This paper covers the revision process of the journal, as well as details about the first *Architecture Asia* forum, the Thailand Contemporary Architecture Forum, with the hope of advancing new models to promote regional interaction between ARCASIA member institutes to improve the international influence of young Asian architects, and to enhance professional communications between Asia and the world.

Keywords

Asian Architecture, Thailand contemporary architecture, ARCASIA, Asian discourse.

Figure 1
A selection of published magazine issues

1. *Architecture Asia* in Progress

Since its founding more than thirty years ago, *Architecture Asia* has always been dedicated to the objectives of the Architects Regional Council Asia (ARCASIA): "To foster and maintain professional contacts, mutual cooperation and assistance among member institutes, to represent architects of the member institutes at national and international levels, to promote the recognition of the architect's role in society, and to promote the development and education of architects and the architectural profession in their service to society," among other things. This journal has been professionally acclaimed and has attracted a wide range of enthusiastic readers within the globe, for its commitment to the development of contemporary architecture in Asia, as well as its focus on professional exchanges among architects. At the end of 2019, through the joint decision of the executive committee of the publication and the council of ARCASIA, the Architectural Society of China (ASC) and Tongji University were designated as the co-organizers of the journal, with an editorial office stationed in the College of Architecture and Urban Planning, Tongji University.

As we enter the third decade of the twenty-first century, with the ever-changing trends of contemporary Asian architecture, key topics such as urbanization, locality, and cross-cultural exchanges still remain the subjects of heated discussion, but with new terms like climate change, information technology, and artificial intelligence fast emerging to join the discussion. Such circumstances pose challenges to expanding the sphere of today's discussions around Asian architecture. *Architecture Asia*, as the showcase of Asian architectural philosophies, therefore, requires a need for revision, in terms of content, structure,

expression, and demonstration method. The past three years have witnessed the innovative improvements of the journal's content, structure, and work model designed by ASC and the editorial department of Tongji University, based on the current journal positioning and readership network.

1.1 Innovation of Content and Structure

1.1.1 Expand horizons—from architecture to cities
Since the 1980s, the discourse of Asian architects has gradually extended from the built environment of individual buildings to the large-scale realm of cities, which is reflected in the systematic shaping of urban external space. In the context of the urbanization of Asia in the twentieth century, Asian architects have gradually taken the role of improving and guiding the urban living environment beyond innovation in architectural design. From 2020 to 2022, *Architecture Asia*'s issues were presented in a thematic form, covering various topics related to urbanization, urban regeneration, and sustainable urban development. For example, the September 2021 issue themed "Urban Regeneration," focused on urban problems in Asia driven by Western thoughts, international investments, and other external effects. It also highlighted how the awakening of the Asian consciousness has been shaping Asian cities by steering them from "rapid construction" to "organic regeneration."

1.1.2 Academic thinking—from design to concept
Architecture Asia has been aimed at professional architects since it was first established, focusing on the iteration and communication of Asian architectural design works. The types of

contemporary Asian architectural design works continue to expand, and their quality continues to improve, thereby laying the foundation for the formation of the "Asian architecture" discourse system. And as new social issues continue to emerge at the same time, the philosophy behind these works is, gradually becoming more targeted and systematic. The journal proposes themes that are opposite but also connected, such as "Globalization and Locality" (June 2022) and "Renovation and Innovation" (September 2022), hoping to inspire dialectical thinking about Asian architecture, and to gradually establish observation systems at both academic and practical levels, starting from a point-like discourse, so as to promote the construction of the academic network of Asian architecture.

1.1.3 Enhance communication—from space to culture

For a long time, emphasis has been put more on the geographical concept of "Asian architecture" than on its cultural concept, without interactions between material and cultural features of space. Many scholars hope to define the "Asianness" of Asian architecture. In fact, whether Asianness can be given a precise definition still remains to be seen, requiring long-term exploration; but it's obvious that cultural characteristics should be interpreted at multidimensional levels. The journal hopes to improve the communication capacity of *Architecture Asia* as a cultural carrier—on the one hand, to break through the single-standard evaluation system of architectural works to build global recognition and consensus on contemporary Asian architecture, and on the other hand, to attract a wider range of authors and readers through cultural popularization and to introduce professional architectural knowledge to the public. In the process of revision, the journal hopes to transform itself from a traditional paper media to an expanded form, as a platform for international exchanges and knowledge spreading through forums, exhibitions, new media (the internet/Facebook/WeChat), and other channels.

1.2 Restructuring of Workflow

Innovation in the content and structure of the journal requires a more efficient planning and operation mode to ensure timeliness, so the workflow of the journal has been rebuilt.

1.2.1 Personnel development—form a network of academic editors and attract young ones

Aligned with the principles of professionalism and academic quality, the journal has formed a network of academic editors around its core editorial committee. To encourage regional fairness, as well as a global perspective, authoritative architects and architectural scholars are recommended from the combined selection of internationally renowned scholars concerned with Asian issues and recommendations from member institutes of ARCASIA, along with relevant observers from architectural media, exhibition curation, and other fields. The final list consisting of twenty-five academic editors is verified, revised, and voted through by the editorial board.

In addition, in order to deliver cutting-edge, rich content, and to respond to ARCASIA's focus on young architects, the journal also launched a call-to-join in 2023, targeted at young academic editors. To expand the network to young scholars who have long-term collaboration or contribution experience with the journal, this call-to-join is extended to other Asian countries and regions, such as India, Thailand, Malaysia, Hong Kong, and Macau, and aims to

gradually also include groups of young scholars in the United States, Spain, Switzerland, and other regions.

1.2.2 Promotion pathways—international distribution and new media channels

Since its establishment, *Architecture Asia* has been committed to print media. However, to strengthen the journal's international reputation and influence, and also considering today's widespread and real-time network of information dissemination, a revision is needed—which looks to upgrade the issue framework and build the journal's website and social media platforms, like Facebook, so as to be able to publish real-time updates about new publications and forums and upcoming issues, and track and report on the various activities of ARCASIA and its member associations, as well as open global subscription and selling channels. In the past, paper journals were distributed through the internal channels of ARCASIA, as well as through subscriptions by universities, institutions, and firms/practices. After the revision, the journal hopes to broaden its international distribution and subscription channels. Other than the existing readership base established through its print subscriptions, the journal is also published electronically and distributed by partnering with The Images Publishing Group, an international authoritative publisher. Both the print and electronic versions are currently available on Amazon and Words & Visuals Press, with a total of 400 copies sold online, per issue.

1.2.3 Revision plan of 2023—dual track mode of "forum + issue"

To further increase the visibility of the member associations of ARCASIA, beginning 2023, the journal adopted a "2+1+1" model for soliciting and commissioning papers, which denotes two national (regional) issues, one themed issue, and one special issue on the ARCASIA Awards for Architecture. The national (regional) issues focus on the contemporary architectural development of a specific region, gradually building the discourse structure of contemporary Asian architecture "from one to many" levels to provide the possibility of research and "mapping" of contemporary Asian architecture. The annual thematic issue enhances the depth and activity of discussions, so as to respond to the current "hot" topics of Asian contemporary architectural culture. The journal will also organize and conduct forums in line with the themes of the national (regional) issues, inviting regional architects to share their practices and reflections. Such forums' real-time nature will inspire broader discussions and also generate international publicity of the national (regional) issues.

2. Thailand Contemporary Architecture Forum

2.1 Opportunity

The 2023 revision plan for *Architecture Asia* was communicated to member associations via the council of ARCASIA, sparking their attention and participation. The Association of Siamese Architects under Royal Patronage (ASA) took the first initiative to recommend architects Jenchieh Hung and Kulthida Songkittipakdee as guest editors; they have long been active players in the practice of Thai architecture, as well as in generating media content in publications on Thai architecture. As experienced veterans in publishing journals, they have also solicited special issues on contemporary Thai architecture in journals like *art4d* and *World Architecture*. Thanks to

Figure 2
Group photo of Architecture
Asia Forum Series: Thailand
Contemporary Architecture

Figure 3
The diverse locations of the
Advisory Board members

SOUTH KOREA
USA PAKISTAN
HONG KONG, CHINA
SINGAPORE
JAPAN MALAYSIA INDIA
MAINLAND, CHINA BELGIUM
UK MACAU, CHINA

their experience and keen insight on the Thai architectural climate, *Architecture Asia*'s first issue for 2023 on contemporary Thai architecture, titled "Local Progressive—Thailand Contemporary Architecture" advanced smoothly.

The first *Architecture Asia* forum was also themed "Thailand Contemporary Architecture." This forum is the first event of the Architecture Asia Forum Series, co-hosted by *Architecture Asia* and ASA, with full support from ARCASIA and ASC, with the aim to express the new tendencies of Thailand's contemporary architecture. Since September 2022, Thailand architects Jenchieh Hung and Kulthida Songkittipakdee have been invited as guest editors and forum convenors, and they are familiar with the development of the contemporary architecture of Thailand, and are well connected with architects active in practical design there. For this first issue in 2023, they proposed to initiate the discussion from the dual perspectives of "academia" and "practice," to show the trends of contemporary architecture in Thailand in a comprehensive and in-depth manner.

2.2 Process

On December 3, 2022, the Thailand Contemporary Architecture Forum was held online. ARCASIA President, Dr. Abu Sayeed M. Ahmed, ASA President, Chana Sumpalung, and Professor Wu Jiang, editor in chief of *Architecture Asia*, delivered opening addresses successively. Associate Professor Zhou Minghao, the managing editor of the journal, and Assistant Professor Wang Yanze, the executive editor, were moderators. The ten groups of Thai pioneer architects who presented at the forum delivered impressive speeches and featured their design projects; five scholars and architects from Asia and Europe

involved in the panel discussion also shared their academic viewpoints. The forum lasted about five hours and was open to global audiences through a free online livestream on YouTube, attracting nearly 5,000 online attendees.

The event gave a platform to Thai architects to share their design projects and enabled the expression and sharing of the current status and trends of contemporary architecture in Thailand, from the perspectives of climate adaptation, local materials, traditional craftsmanship, and community integration, as well as new economy and technologies—including business logic, performance-driven initiatives, ecological adaptability, and high-density construction. In the panel discussion, the five scholars discussed and analyzed contemporary Thailand architecture from the perspectives of "globalization and locality," "urban and rural," "spontaneous regionalism," and "traditional context and modern interpretation," among other contexts and angles.

2.3 Reflections

The keyword "Thai-ness" was repeatedly mentioned in the forum's discussions. The projects of the ten groups of architects fully exhibited rich levels of "Thai-ness," however, the concept's extensions and connotations are still growing and expanding. In the first half of the twentieth century, the modernist architectural practice in Thailand was stimulated by the introduction of Western modernist architectural philosophies, but it surprisingly did not imitate any Western styles. In recent years, Thai architecture has been frequently taking to the international stage, not by pursuing certain "features or types" and conforming to Thai architecture, but by attracting global attention through unconventional and unique architectural designs. Such a liberating and casual design

Figure 4
Official website of
Architecture Asia

style on the one hand may originate from the enthusiastic and free personalities of architects in tropical upbringing, but on the other, may come from the inclusiveness of Thai culture since ancient times. From urban landscape to architectural forms, architects in Thai cities are entitled with great freedom and possibilities at institutional and spatial levels.

3. Summary

The Thailand Contemporary Architecture Forum proposed several key topics worth discussing, such as "Nature"—responding to climate change and environmental control in tropical areas; "Surroundings"—coping with increasingly complex urban and rural environments; "Culture"—responding to the constantly emerging social and cultural issues related to historical traditions, information technology, spatial justice, and such aspects. These could become the starting points for the next round of discussions on contemporary architecture in Thailand, and even in Asia.

As an observer media, the responsibility of *Architecture Asia* is to inspire a new round of exploration, which means our perspective is not to deliver conclusive comments, but to find inspiring beginnings. We look forward to more architects and scholars from Asia and the world joining the discussions of *Architecture Asia*.

Nurse Dormitory, Chulalongkorn Memorial Hospital

Looking up to the top from drop-off area

Architect firm: Plan Architect
Principal architect: Nitisak Chobdamrongtham, Apichai Apichatanon, Wara Jithpratuck
Design team: Naphasorn Kiatwinyoo, Nathida Sornchumni
Location: Patumwan, Bangkok, Thailand
Area: 32,000 square meters
Completion date: November 2020
Photography: Panoramic Studio

The nurses' dormitory at Chulalongkorn Memorial Hospital (the new dormitory), also known by the royal name, Nawarachupatum, assigned by Her Royal Highness Princess Maha Chakri Sirindhorn, is a dormitory for nurses working at Chulalongkorn Memorial Hospital of the Thai Red Cross Society. The building has twenty-six floors with 523 rooms. Most of the rooms accommodate two people and include various facilities, such as a living area, library, pantry/kitchenette, bathroom, and multipurpose room.

The project site originally contained four existing buildings that housed doctors' and nurses' dormitories, three of which were high-rise buildings. The new dormitory replaces the low-rise building in the middle of the site, which was demolished to construct the new dormitory. A nearby main road serves as a thoroughfare often used by vehicles.

The design and layout of the new dormitory interacts with the three high-rise buildings, such that an enclosed courtyard is created, which is separated from the crowded, busy atmosphere of the hospital. The ground floor of the building is an open space connecting the main road with the courtyard, and presents as a metaphorical gateway into this quiet and peaceful residential area.

The design team's research for the project revealed that most of the dormitory's resident nurses prefer naturally ventilated rooms to air-conditioned rooms. Nurturing varieties of gardens that included trees and plants along the balcony was also popular among them. The main concept of the design strives to serve these needs. The design team's analysis of a typical dormitory with a double-load corridor arrangement revealed that such layouts usually lack natural light and often have poor indoor ventilation. To solve this, two sides of the new building are separated to make two single-load corridor arrangements, with a gap in the middle. This design allows more natural light into the corridor and creates a ventilation chimney in the middle of the building , which facilitates ventilation from basement to the rooftop. A large air channel is designed on the first floor and center of the building, as well as the rooftop, to create a stack effect, drawing air from the basement up to the top. The design of the air channel on the façade was inspired by the "Una-Lome Daeng," the original design of the logo of the Thai Red Cross Society.

The design of the rooms features a double-door entrance made up of a solid main door and an insect screen. When the main door and the window at the balcony are opened, the air from the corridor can flow through the room.

The typical room layout is divided into two parts. The first part, adjacent to the corridor, is a shared space that includes a pantry/kitchenette and bathroom, with a sliding door to separate the area from the bedroom. The sliding door creates privacy for the residents in the bedroom, should they decide to leave the main door open to allow natural air to flow through the room. The second part is the bedroom, which is shared by both residents. The beds are placed on the opposite sides of the room, so as to create a private space for each resident; a walkway in the middle leads to the balcony.

As the dormitory is close to other nearby buildings, the balcony is designed with a slanted angle to avoid direct sightlines with other buildings, to maintain the privacy of the dormitory's residents and vice versa. The zigzag balcony allows more sunlight into the area, making it conducive to keep plants, small trees, and even dry laundry, or for any other uses residents may have. The design of the railing, with vertical aluminum fins and a sunshade with a perforated aluminum sheet, effectively conceals untidy elements such as a clothes drying rack, washing machine, and the air conditioner condensing unit. Aluminum was selected as the façade material as it is durable and easy to maintain. This unique façade and balcony composition creates a light and shadow texture that reflects the simple systematic design of the building, while also concealing the various functional requirements of the users.

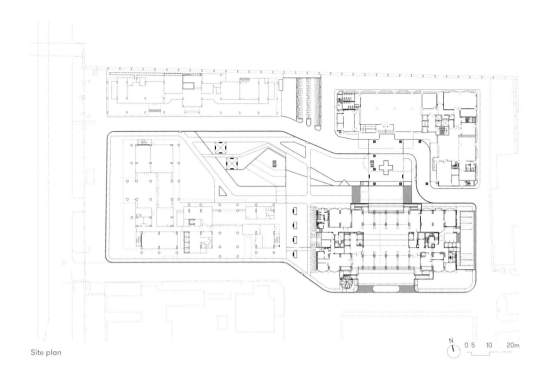

Site plan

N 0 5 10 20m

View of the building from courtyard

Common area deck on the fifteenth floor

Common area deck on the thirteenth floor

View of the bedroom zone

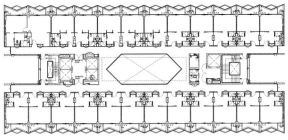

Twenty-sixth-floor plan

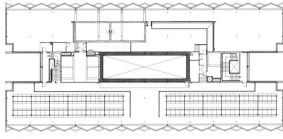

Rooftop floor plan

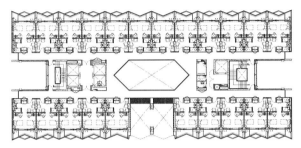

Fourth-floor plan

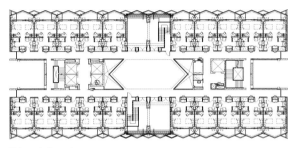

Thirteenth-floor plan

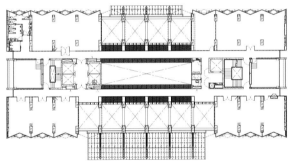

Second-floor plan

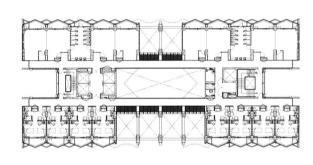

Third-floor plan

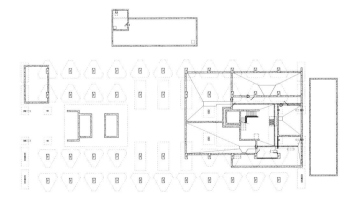

Basement floor plan

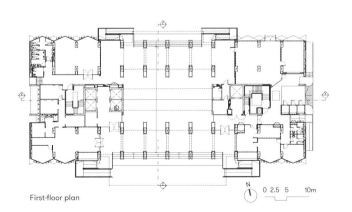

First-floor plan

0 2.5 5 10m

View from courtyard

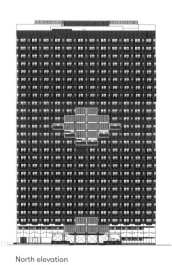
North elevation

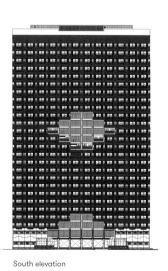
South elevation

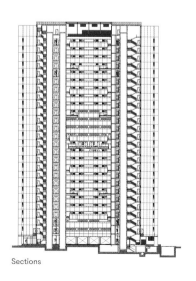
Sections

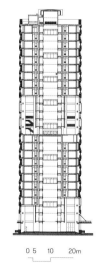
0 5   10   20m

Sarnsara Learning Center

The auditorium and dormitory building facing the lake

Architect firm: Architects 49 Limited (A49)
Principal architect: Prabhakorn Vadanyakul, Somkiat Lochindapong
Design team: Narongwit Areemit, Thanarat Karnpool
Location: Ratchaburi Province, Thailand
Area: 16,592 square meters
Completion date: January 2020
Photography: Nattakit Jeerapatmaitree

The design of Sarnsara Learning Center in Ratchaburi Province, Thailand, integrates Muang Thai Life Assurance's core values: "The M Powered C—Customer Centric, Creativity, Commitment to Success, Collaboration, and Caring." In the spirit of Muang Thai Life Assurance's collaborative culture, the center's design encourages interaction and the exchange of ideas between users, providing spaces for discussions and casual meetings, facilitating the company's belief that new products can emerge from anybody in the organization.

A triangle modular configuration enables users to create different rooms to suit a variety of purposes, from seminars and meetings to group discussions and workshops, reflecting the company's customer centric values. This triangular module is also applied to spaces for outdoor activities. In line with the theme, the triangle shape is utilized in the ceiling systems of semi-outdoor spaces to draw light in from the skylight. Combined with hues of the company's brand color, the resulting atmosphere can be likened to sitting in the shade of a fuchsia tree.

An oval-shaped auditorium reflects, as well as promotes, the idea of a happy community, and the overall atmosphere creates a collaborative work culture. Facilities in the center include a 1,000-seat auditorium, training rooms of various sizes that can accommodate up to 200 people, and seventy-three guestrooms. Residential units are secluded from the street, with views of the lake, offering privacy and a place for relaxation.

Incorporating characteristic elements inspired by renowned local earthenware, a refreshing and informal atmosphere that is well received by both locals and training participants is created.

Muang Thai Life Assurance also places great importance on energy efficiency and environmental protection. In line with this advocacy of sustainability and environmental values, the learning center was reviewed against U.S.'s Green Building Council's Leadership in Energy and Environmental Design (LEED) standard and received a Gold certification in October 2020. The center's architectural and engineering design enable a 26 percent reduction in energy consumption, compared to many other facilities of a similar size and function. This was achieved, in part, by employing renewable energy systems, such as rooftop solar panels. Daylight analysis and computational simulation were used to determine the best design and location for the skylight in the learning area, so as to create a naturally lit space which reduces energy consumption during the day. The learning area is also naturally ventilated, minimizing the need for air conditioning. The landscape architecture, with its green areas and large ponds, is designed to reduce heat, as well as the Mean Radiant Temperature (MRT) surrounding the project.

With its nature surroundings, its relaxed environment, and its consideration toward energy efficiency, lifecycle, and maintenance, the Sarnsara Learning Center is imbued with the core value of caring.

Walkway approach to the training center and auditorium

53

1. Learning and training center
2. Auditorium
3. Residential zone
4. Parking

Site plan

0 5 10   30m

The main buildings and accommodation complexes surround the central water catchment area

Outside the training center building

Front view of training center

Corridor between the auditorium and training center

Sunlight shines through the skylight roof

In the training center's hall

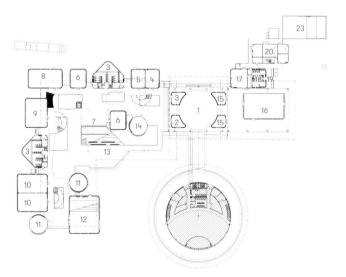

First-floor plan of the learning and training center

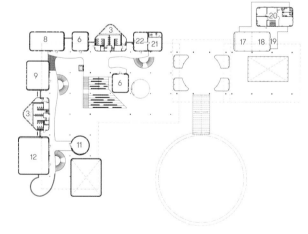

Second-floor plan of the learning and training center

1.   Lobby
2.   Front office
3.   WC+support function
4.   Academic office
5.   Meeting room
6.   Seminar hall (size S)
7.   Bag deposit
8.   Computer room I
9.   Computer room II
10. Seminar hall (size M)
11. Activity room
12. Seminar hall (size L)
13. Multipurpose plaza
14. Lounge/library
15. VIP dining area
16. Canteen
17. Kitchen
18. WC
19. Service corridor
20. Support building
21. CEO room
22. Executive room
23. Chiller room

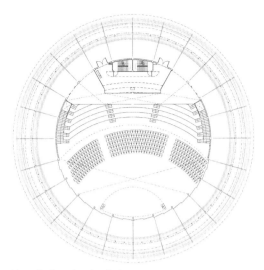

Mezzanine floor plan of auditorium

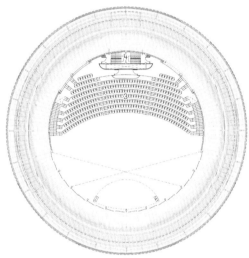

Second-floor plan of auditorium

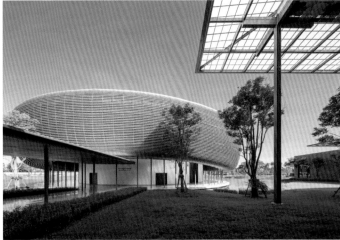

Corridor connecting to the auditorium

Auditorium interior

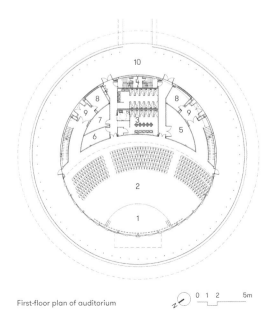

First-floor plan of auditorium

1.   Main stage
2.   Flat floor auditorium
3.   Sloped floor auditorium
4.   Emergency exit
5.   Backstage area
6.   Control room
7.   EE and Comms room
8.   Reception
9.   Entrance foyer
10. Exterior foyer
11. Restrooms
12. AHU room
13. Janitor storage

Side view of training center

Side view of waterfront and auditorium

Elevations of training center

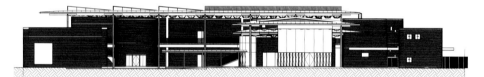

Section of training center

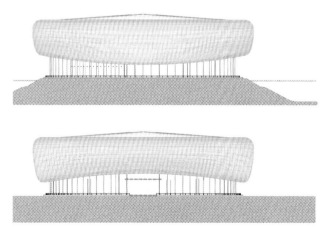

Elevations of auditorium

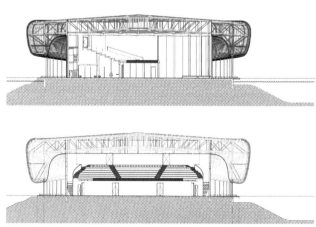

Sections of auditorium

SYC Office

Entrance view

Architect firm: Duangrit Bunnag Architect Limited (DBALP)
Principal architect: Duangrit Bunnag
Design team: Artirin Piripun, Prinpon Boonkham, Jiratchaya Kuegoonlittiwong
Location: Pak Kret, Nonthaburi, Thailand
Area: 3,075 square meters
Completion date: November 2021
Photography: Wison Tungthunya

The building structure is made of steel and concrete slabs, which create a long-span opening. The façade is composed of glass, U-Glass, and precast concrete to maintain the clean line of the building. The exterior wall of the building is lined with precast concrete slabs, leaving a small light gap, so as to maintain privacy from neighboring buildings. The floor-to-floor height measures 4.10 meters, which allows enough room to contain all mechanical functions within the ceiling, while imparting a spacious feel to workspaces, creating a pleasant environment to work in.

This five-story office building compound with four business office units, canteen, event hall, three meeting rooms, and a director's quarter on the top floor is located at Pak Kret, Nonthaburi, Thailand, and designed in white, with a clean line articulation that interacts with a green area and a water body.

The open space, placed in the heart of the compound, shares the attractive nature designed around the building with the building's users. It also allows gentle breezes to pass through the corridor and other common areas, facilitating good ventilation throughout the building. This empowers the complex with energy efficiency through static space.

Drop-off and entrance view

Office space

Back view

View of small open space from connecting bridge

60

Meeting room space

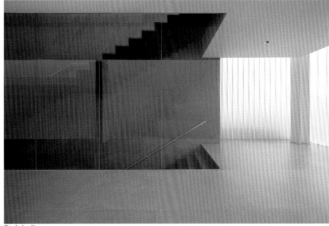

Stair hall

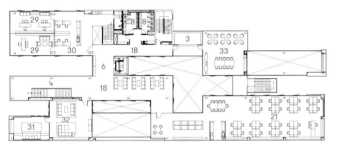

Fourth-floor plan

Fifth-floor plan

Second-floor plan

Third-floor plan

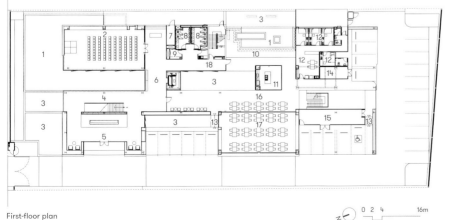

First-floor plan

1.	Reflecting pool	18.	Hall
2.	Meeting room	19.	Waiting area
3.	Garden	20.	Document room
4.	Stair hall	21.	Office
5.	Entrance hall	22.	Pantry area
6.	Lift hall	23.	Executive room
7.	Pump room	24.	Director's unit
8.	Toilet	25.	Executive toilet
9.	Service room	26.	Administration room
10.	Terrace	27.	Relaxation room
11.	Food preparation area	28.	Library
12.	Helper's room	29.	Double executive room
13.	Accessibility ramp	30.	Secretary area
14.	Pump room	31.	Sanctum
15.	Electrical room	32.	Living room
16.	Outdoor canteen	33.	Executive dining room
17.	Canteen	34.	Roof

0 2 4   16m

Library

Library terrace

Elevations

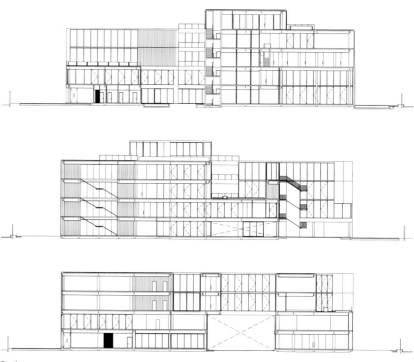

Sections

No Sunrise No Sunset Pavilion

A glossy geometric aluminum composite reflects the surrounding natural rocky landscape. The juxtaposition of materials and shapes is enhanced, while accompanying each other harmoniously

Architect firm: Walllasia
Design team: Suriya Umpansiriratana (Architect), Kamin Lertchaiprasert (Artist)
Location: Ao Nang Beach, Krabi Province, Thailand
Area: 50 square meters
Completion date: October 2018
Photography: Spaceshift Studio

To convey the concept of the work, Kamin Lertchaiprasert draws inspiration from the story of Yai Sa, who awaits the return of her love who left her on a quest to search for the ultimate truth, promising her that he would return to her once he finds it.

And so, every day, she stands at the same point at which he left her side, waiting for him.

What is the ultimate truth? And where is it? Is it extrinsic; or is it what is already in our mind? What is love, mercy, change, death, emptiness, and oneness?

A collaboration between Walllsia and Lertchaiprasert, the No Sunrise No Sunset Pavilion, which was constructed for the Thailand Biennale 2018, was a creation of fine art represented through architecture.

Lertchaiprasert, who avidly questions the philosophies of life and truth, pursues his artistic practice as a means to discover and explore the relationships between and beyond those two words. The evolution of his practice over the last thirty years, from an interest of self to exploring relationships, has resulted in various projects that involve elements of collaboration, participation, and learning together. His projects are referred to as "life-specific" rather than site-specific, with an approach that combines the contextualization of the physicality of the space and the spiritual aspects of life, with the aim to convert site-specificity into what can be seen as a condition of universality.

For this collaboration project with Walllasia, the name No Sunrise No Sunset was chosen to embody how the sun stays in the same place, neither rising or setting, but it is in fact the earth that revolves, making it appear to move, which symbolizes that people see the world in the way that we want to, rather than how it actually is. So, often, one's perception forms their reality. If we were to see the world objectively, the way it truly is, we would see beauty and the virtue of its nature.

This project represents the parallel plane between the world in its ultimate truth and the illusionary world. It also creates the awareness of timeless moments and an objective perspective with no "self" attachments. That is the connection between inner and outer space (subjective and objective), and "you" and "me."

Inspired by the prehistoric conditions in the caves of Krabi Province, Thailand, the design team created a cave-like architecture in which prehistoric human conditions are highlighted. In the cave stood a sculpture of Yai Sa, presenting a symbol of love and devotion, patiently waiting.

Half of the floor plan is formed by a watery floor to connect the pavilion to the sea and also divide the singular space. The mirror exterior reflects a minimal, contemporary style that also blends the installation with the surrounding environment—a hidden cliffside location popular among locals and tourists seeking refuge from the hustle of the resort town.

Given the time constraint to complete the project, a prefabricated steel frame was used to construct the pavilion in just under twenty-eight days. All the materials used were sourced locally or from nearby areas.

The No Sunrise No Sunset Pavilion was not created to respond only to Krabi and Ao Nang; it can be placed anywhere, to frame views in any area or region, because, as you know, "The sun stays in the same place, but it is the world that is spinning around."

The glossy façade reflects the surrounding nature while hiding its content within another dimension, which is only exposed through the approach sequences

The site, which marks the end of the path, used to be a corner where tourists came to watch the sunset, and is quite challenging to find. The work stands like a piece of art and presents an experience likened with approaching art

Nature and moments in different frames

The cantilevered structure, the reflection of the surrounding nature, and the different-similar effects solicit questions that align with the Lertchaiprasert's concept, communicated through the sculpture *Yai Sa* inside the pavilion

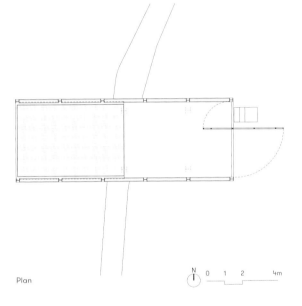

Plan

N   0   1   2   4m

The vast sea connects through the reflection of the water at sunset, into a rectangular box where a sculpture by Lertchaiprasert of an old *Yai Sa* stands. Again, there is the implication of waiting for something

The difference and relationship between artistic form and nature

Elevation

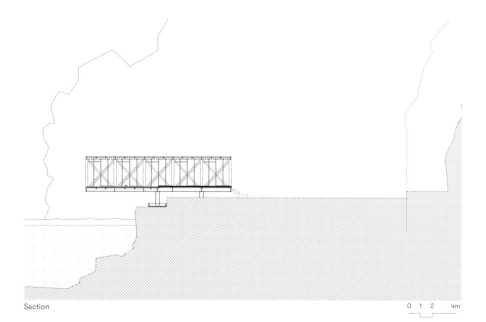

Section

0 1 2   4m

Elephant World

Elephant World is located on a barren site that was once a reserved forest, situating the project on the abandoned land instead of clearing trees to make way for the buildings

Architect firm: Bangkok Project Studio
Principal architect: Boonserm Premthada
Design team: Boonserm Premthada,
Nathan Mehl
Location: Surin Province, Thailand
Area: 14,040 square meters
Completion date: September 2020
Photography: Spaceshift Studio

Elephant World is a big project composed of three buildings: the Brick Observation Tower, the Cultural Courtyard, and the Elephant Museum.

Elephants have a special status in Thailand. They are the stars of grand royal ceremonies and were also war animals for the kings throughout the country's ancient history. In addition to being revered and respected, the relationship between elephants and Thai people is unique and elephants are treated as family members rather than pets or labor. This bond is perhaps strongest in the Ban Ta Klang village of the ethnic Kui in Surin Province, northeastern Thailand. For many centuries, the community has lived with elephants, forming their way of life with them, from birth to death. The two can hardly be separated.

Once lush greenery, the forest of Surin was destroyed over the last half of the twentieth century to cultivate cash crops, resulting in the Kui and their elephants suffering extreme droughts, as well as the shortage of food and medicinal plants, which the forest once provided. Deprived of sustenance, the Kui and their elephants were displaced to tourist towns, degraded to begging for food, or working in elephant camps, many with unsuitable living conditions.

Elephant Museum forms part of Elephant World, a project initiated by the local government to bring the Kui and their elephants back to their homeland, with suitable living conditions tailored for the elephants. Apart from architectural elements, the museum also features audio snippets from the villagers and more than 200 elephants living in the village. These recordings provide an understanding of the long-established familial relationship between the Kui and their elephants and also reveal the strong disapproval the Kui have toward the cruelty of animal exploitation, while also sharing their hopes for the future.

Amid a vast treeless landscape, curved walls of varying heights sprout from the ground, seemingly opening the building up to elephant-size visitors. The walls slope and cross one another, revealing gaps that lead visitors to the inside, where courtyards of different shapes and sizes open up from four exhibition galleries. Some are filled with small pools, and some with reddish earth, just like the landscape outside. Different scales of outdoor paths, sheltered spaces, and open courtyards recall the elements of the area—from elephants, humans, and their houses to the ponds they both bathe in and the mud baths the playful elephants enjoy.

Sunlight is an essential element in the design as it helps portray the typical daily Kui life that usually unfolds under the sun. Rooms and paths are brightly lit by sunlight in certain areas and dimmed in others. The shadow and light effects change throughout the day, depending on the angle of the sun. Exhibitions may be staged within the courtyards or on the exterior walls. Inside the galleries, one may only find seats to rest and look out toward the displays outside, while they reflect on the coexistence of the two species.

Over 480,0000 fired clay bricks made by hand from loam found in the area using a technique passed down through generations were used in the construction of the museum. In a town where job opportunities are few, the construction process created jobs and income for the locals, while increasing the value of often overlooked local material. The museum strives to empower the Kui and their elephants and end their struggling for decades away from home. It also hopes to empower the people of Surin. Its programs aims to encourage them to take pride in their heritage and restore the dignity of their beloved elephants once again.

From the outside, the building appears plain. The roof is low-lying, in harmony with the surrounding village

Inside, the generous height of the roof and the expanse of the cultural courtyard reveals itself

Curved walls at varying heights sprout from the vast landscape. Some slope down to the ground, acting like a door that opens to elephant-size visitors

Eventually, the forest shall return to the land, and the building will peek through only at its apex

The steel mesh staircases at the center of the tower attenuate the sunlight from above

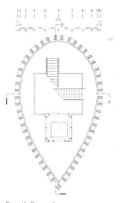
Fourth-floor plan

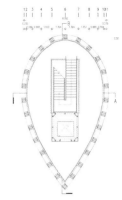
Fifth-floor plan

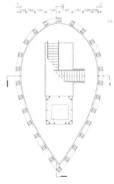
Second-floor plan

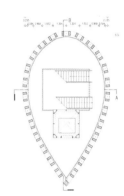
Third-floor plan

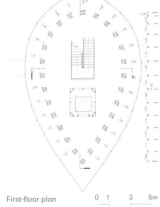
First-floor plan

0 1   3   5m

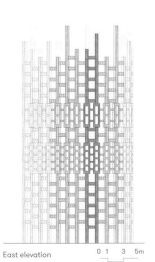
East elevation   0 1   3   5m

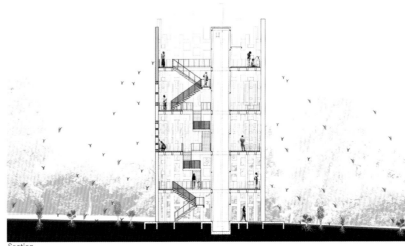
Section

The 70×100 meters sloping roof spans a large ground where cultural events and religious ceremonies—such as those commemorating the birth to the death of humans and elephants—can take place

Approaching the building, the inside is hidden from view. The steepness of the mounds creates a unique transition from the outside to the inside

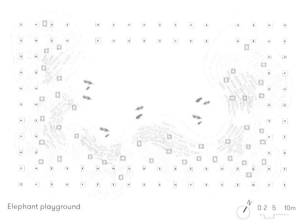

Elephant playground

N 0 2 5 10m

A Building the mounds meant digging a new rainwater collection pond

B A seedling in a plant box will one day grow through the roof opening, providing shade and food

C Mining basalt for the building helped create another groundwater source nearby

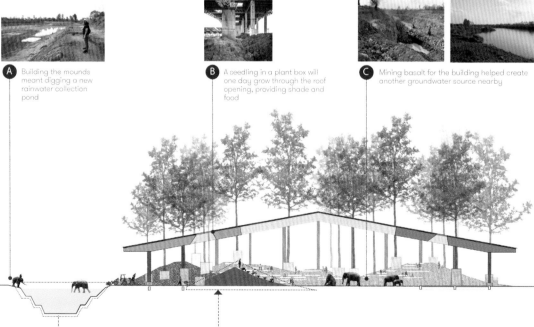

Different scales of outdoor paths, sheltered spaces, and open courtyards recall the elements of the area—from elephants, humans, their houses, and the ponds they both bathe in to the mud and dirt bath the playful elephants enjoy

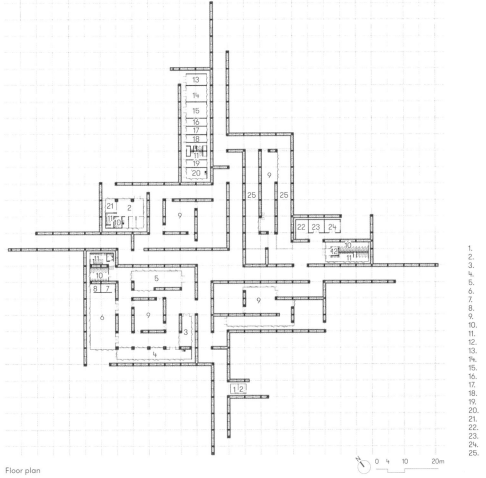

1. Box office
2. Staff room
3. Gift shop
4. Restaurant and beverage store
5. Library
6. Seminar room (accommodates 100)
7. Speakers' lounge
8. Control room
9. Exhibition hall
10. Female restroom
11. Male restroom
12. Accessible restroom
13. Storage room
14. Carpentry room
15. Art room
16. Technician's room
17. Security guard's room
18. System control room
19. Housekeeper's room
20. Staff pantry
21. Meeting room (staff)
22. Pump room
23. Electrical room
24. UPS room
25. Pond

Floor plan

N   0 4   10   20m

Over 480,0000 fired clay bricks were made by hand from loam found in the area using a technique passed down through generations. The construction of Elephant Museum created jobs and income for the locals, while increasing the value of often overlooked local material

Brick walls of various heights overlap one another as one walks through the interior; each side of a room is surrounded by courtyards of different sizes and shapes

Courtyards of different shapes and sizes open up from the four exhibition galleries, with some filled with small pools and others with reddish earth, just like the landscape outside

The Commons Saladaeng

The Commons Saladaeng is located in a lush, green neighborhood in the middle of Bangkok's CBD area

Architect firm: Department of ARCHITECTURE Co.
Principal architect: Amata Luphaiboon,
Twitee Vajrabhaya Teparkum
Design team: Chanlika Boonpha,
Tanadetch Mahapolsirikun,
Monthon Patcharapunyapong,
Supavit Junsompitsiri
Location: Bangrak, Thailand
Area: 3,000 square meters
Completion date: January 2020
Photography: Spaceshift Studio

The Commons Saladaeng is the second development from The Commons family. It hosts a variety of F&B outlets, along with other services and activities. The project is nestled in a vibrant neighborhood in Bangkok, Thailand, known as Saladaeng, which translates to "a red pavilion." The name comes from a small train station in the neighborhood with a red gabled roof that stood distinctly in the middle of the rice field a hundred years ago, as part of the first railway line of the country. The design of The Commons Saladaeng pays homage to this little-known history of the neighborhood.

Red, rubber corrugated sheets have been chosen as the main architectural material for two reasons: their crimson color, and how the corrugated surface ties back to the character of the roof of the old train station. The clear and the red transparent corrugated sheets, which have different levels of visual transparency, add a layer of complexity to the simple architectural form of the building. Eight small gables, reminiscent in scale of those in the past, suitably accommodate present-day requirements for wider interior spaces through a specially designed M-shape roof structure that reconciles the sentimental scale of the past and the operational scale of the present.

The best feature of the site is a large 15-meter-tall ficus tree in the front. The building façade forms a concave curve that recedes from the tree to minimize any disturbance to its branches and roots, while emphasizing the tree itself as the focal point of the space. The middle volume is carved out as an open-air public space that is orientated toward the tree. The ficus tree also helps to screen out the visually incongruous context across the street, while adding a level of privacy and intimacy to the space within.

The high-density CBD of Saladaeng leaves the people working there craving for an open-air area with a comfortable microclimate. To that end, almost 30 percent of the building's footprint is tailored to be "Common" ground via a large, welcoming, open-air public space that trails upward to connect the restaurant and coffee bar on the ground floor to the food hall on the second floor, and the multifunction spaces on the third floor. This "Common" ground fuses large steps with platforms, seating, and planting, and is fitted with large industrial fans that generate a "laminar flow" (continuous low-velocity ventilation) through the entire space. This welcoming, generous, well shaded, relaxing, and breezy open-air space effectively provides a range of facilities in a comfortable environment that is suitable for the tropical climate of Bangkok.

The space is designed as a modifiable groundscape through a special pallet unit system that interplays with the cascading steps to transform the space into different configurations for various types of events. This pallet system can be used to create a series of small flat areas throughout the space for setting up booths during a weekend market, or staggered into various steps as seating for a children's event. It can also be arranged to build a small platform for an intimate music performance or construct a large stage to adapt the space into an informal open-air concert venue.

The Commons Saladaeng is an innovative urban lifestyle architecture well-rooted in its local context and climate, with a sense of place. The project is embedded within the neighborhood, and is always adapting itself to serve the life and needs of the community.

The ficus tree is a focal point that provides privacy and intimacy for customers in the "Common" ground

The cascading ground fuses large steps with platforms, seating, and planting

The M-shape roof structure accommodates the need for long-span interior spaces, while maintaining the roof scale of the past

The brightly lit multifunction space on the third floor is welcoming and attractive with string lights that extend through the space

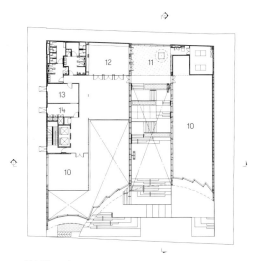

Third-floor plan

Roof plan

1. "Common" ground
2. Grab and go
3. Roast restaurant
4. Roast's kitchen
5. Parking
6. Saladaeng 1 alley
7. Restroom
8. Market
9. Storage room
10. Shop
11. Lawn
12. Multipurpose room
13. Office
14. Control room

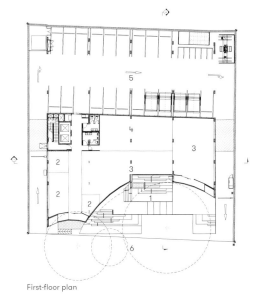

First-floor plan

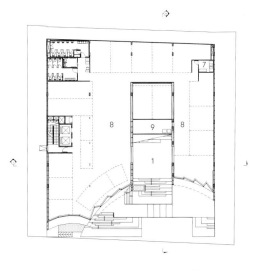

Second-floor plan

N   0 2   5m

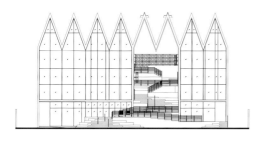
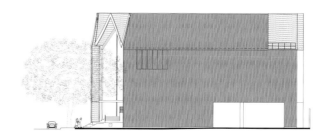

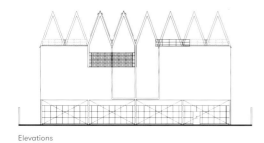
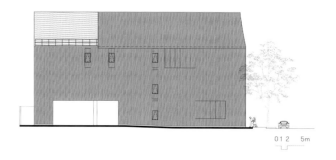

Elevations

0 1 2   5m

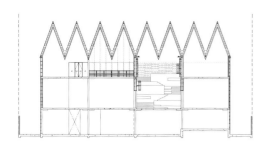

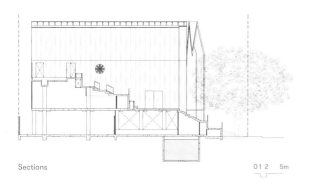

Sections

0 1 2   5m

The red LED light strip gives a striking outline to the façade

Keeree Tara Riverside

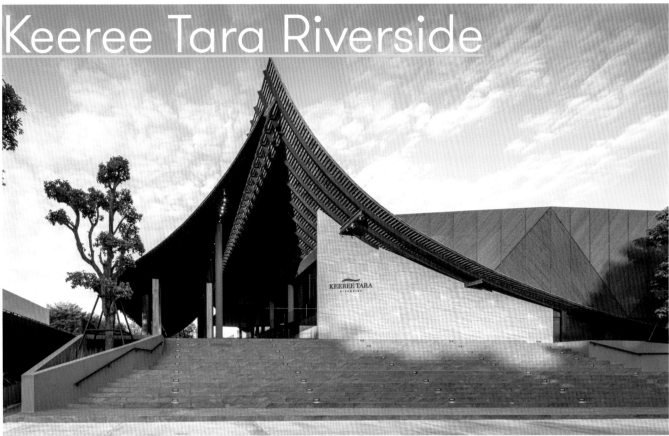

Front view of the restaurant—the main entrance on the second floor, accessed by the staircase that hides the main kitchen on the first floor

Architect firm: IDIN Architects
Principal architect: Jeravej Hongsakul
Design team: Jeravej Hongsakul,
Eakgaluk Sirijariyawat, Sakorn Thongduang,
Wichan Kongnok
Location: Mueang, Kanchanaburi, Thailand
Area: 2,290 square meters
Completion date: May 2022
Photography: DOF Sky|Ground

Keeree Tara is a brand-new restaurant intended as a replacement of its original branch located nearby. The original restaurant is one of the most popular and successful Thai restaurants in Kanchanaburi, Thailand, so the owner decided to maintain a sense of the traditional Thai style reflected on the building, which links the look of the restaurant to the Thai dishes served. The

The staircase leads all visitors to the entry foyer on the second floor.

property is small in size, especially when compared to the required functions of a major restaurant branch; and the restaurant also needed to be able to support large-scale events, such as seminars and weddings. This resulted in having a large commissary kitchen of over a 1,000 square meters in order to fully support any future expansions, as well as the nearby branches. Keeree Tara did not just have to house a large service facility, its location beside the Kwai River also meant that it was crucial to take advantage of the river view and utilize it in both the indoor and outdoor dining zones.

The design process was initiated from the project's limitation—with finding the most functional location for the majority of the services and the commissary kitchen which takes up most of the available space on the first floor. However, this, in combination with a high ceiling, would result in a large building mass that would fill up the space and obstruct the view of the river. Therefore, other usable functions have been placed on the second level, and the kitchen and services behind a large staircase which leads all visitors to the entry foyer on the second floor. The foyer further diverts to the banquet hall on the third level, while also continuing to lead visitors to the dining terrace, which has been designed with alternating levels that gradually lead closer to the river bank, resulting in an area that can be separated into several dining

zones. A banquet hall is placed on the third level to hold functions such as seminars and weddings. The hall is surrounded with a veranda and an additional dining zone with a more elevated view toward the river.

Another important consideration was the incorporation of "Thai-ness" into a large-scale building, which presented the design team with some challenges. Traditionally, large-scale Thai buildings that encompass wide spans are either temples or palaces. Thai houses are traditionally small-scale, and are often collectively placed in clusters. To negotiate this typical standard, the design team incorporates the "sense" and "feel" of Thai architecture into the design, within usable spaces, to highlight and evoke a Thai atmosphere in the restaurant, rather than employ direct proportions or decorative elements from Thai architecture. This interpretation results in a large, curved gable roof that is also functional to the use of the building; the central ridge is offset and centered along the main entrance and slightly tilted, to allow for natural light penetration, creating an axis through a ray of light that extends toward the river. The long side of the gable roof gradually slopes down to reach the floor, which seemingly reduces the gigantic scale of the roof. The slope along the riverside also functions as stairs for users to access the rooftop bar and the roof deck.

The lower-level dining area set close to the river

The view from the entry foyer

The dining terrace designed with alternating levels that gradually lead closer to the river

The walkway to the dining area

The perspective of the corridor from the dining zone to the main entrance

The banquet hall, which is used for functions like weddings and seminars

Third-floor plan

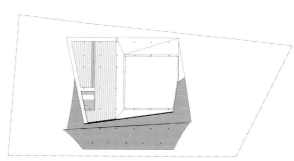

Rooftop floor plan

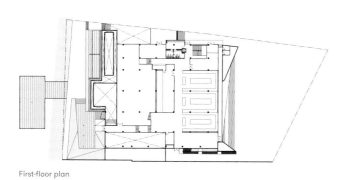

First-floor plan

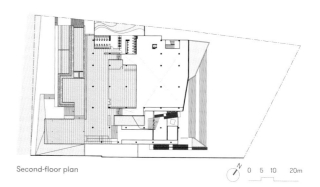

Second-floor plan

N 0 5 10 20m

Keeree Tara is adjacent to the Kwai River

Architecturally, the gable roof helps break the building mass and also aids in visually reducing the building's gigantic scale

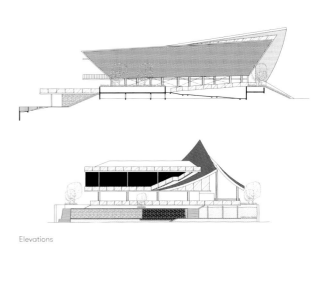

Elevations

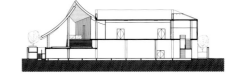

Sections

PANNAR Sufficiency Economic and Agriculture Learning Center

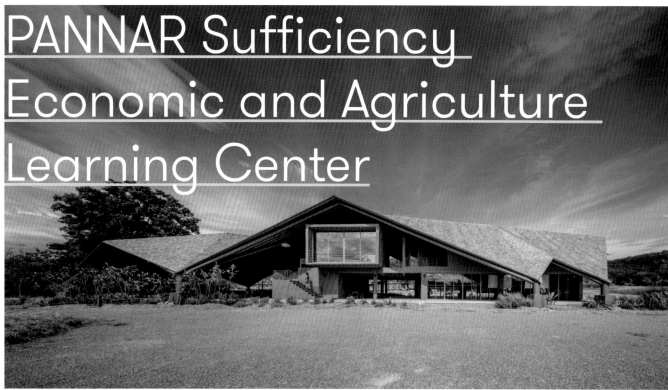

Exterior view the Activity Center from the southeast

Architect firm: Vin Varavarn Architects (VVA)
Principal architect: M. L. Varudh Varavarn
Design team: Jongsarit Jinachan,
Pakamas Nithipong, Nutsiree Wichit
Location: Nakhon Ratchasima, Thailand
Area: 1,191 square meters
Completion date: July 2020
Photography: Ketsiree Wongwan

Over the past decades, the world has encountered increasing challenges that have resulted from the unprecedented rapid rates of technological advancements, increasing social and economic disparities, dangers from natural disasters, the deterioration of natural resources, conflicting values and cultures, and more recently, life-threatening pandemics.

Amid such national and global crises, "Sufficiency Economic Philosophy," elaborated by His Majesty King Bhumibol Adulyadej in 1974, has gained recognition as the beacon of hope guiding Thailand toward an inclusive and sustainable growth model. The philosophy is based on the conviction that sufficiency thinking will strengthen human capabilities with wisdom, ethical values, and morality, and provide immunities to cope with unforeseeable changes and threats in the future.

The Sufficiency Economic and Agriculture Learning Center has been established with the aim to inspire and disseminate the King's Sufficiency Economic Philosophy to the Thai people. The project is located in Nakhon Ratchasima, on a desolate land that was transformed through the government's New Agriculture Model, from an arid and rocky deserted area into rice fields, reservoirs, vegetables gardens, groves of fruit trees and other trees for use, and areas for rearing various types of animals.

The project constructs two main buildings, namely the Activity Center and a building for service and restroom facilities. The Activity Center is a two-story building, designed to accommodate up to 100 people in a variety of functions. The first floor houses a lobby (reception), rooms for seminars and workshops, cafeteria, and a large kitchen. The second floor contains offices and meeting spaces for staff, a control room, and facilities for invited trainers and guest speakers.

In designing the buildings for the project, the architects were challenged to explore the essence of Sufficiency Economy Philosophy as it relates to architecture, especially on whether the buildings needed to conform to the traditional rural dwelling design of bamboo huts and temporary shacks. After much discussion, it was decided that the design would pursue the concept that modern design can use sufficiency thinking principles through transforming local craftsmanship and materials to create modern designs that are attractive, durable, and well suited for the way of life of present day, and also achieve harmony with the environment.

The Activity Center is placed as the landmark among the vast agriculture fields. It is designed as a large and open pavilion to facilitate flexible use, with natural light and ventilation. The large roof, constructed from locally grown bamboo, helps to collect and drain rainwater toward small canals surrounding the building, and redirects the water to irrigate the land before being carried to natural reservoirs that collect water for use during drought seasons. The naturally colored earth walls, created through an experiment with local craftspeople, uses local soil to further project a "sufficiency-thinking mindset" by featuring the adaption of locally available materials and skills for modern uses.

Restroom facilities are designed to overcome the usual concerns of cleanliness and a stifling atmosphere. To facilitate comfort within these facilities, local bricks are used to construct three-dimensional double curved walls. The restroom stalls are located within the outer ring that extend to also delineate the spacious waiting area. The spaces within the patterned brick walls receive ample natural light and promote fresh air ventilation; dampness and moisture build-up is also eliminated and the solid brick walls ensure privacy.

Both buildings reflect the belief that architecture is a living science that must transform and grow with the development of new technology, in response to evolving human needs and behaviors.

Exterior view of the Activity Center from the northwest

Aerial view of the Activity Center

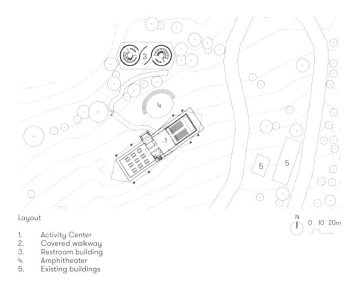

Layout

1.   Activity Center
2.   Covered walkway
3.   Restroom building
4.   Amphitheater
5.   Existing buildings

N   0 10 20m

Interior view of the canteen

Looking toward the meeting room from the balcony

Reception hall

Seminar and indoor workshop room

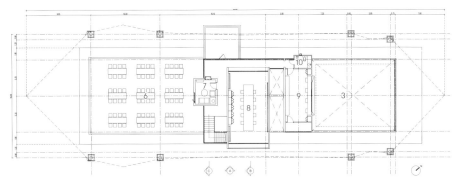

Second-floor plan of Activity Center

1. Reception hall
2. Office
3. Seminar and indoor workshop room
4. Storage
5. Kitchen
6. Canteen and semi-outdoor workshop
7. Guest living room
8. Meeting room
9. Control room
10. Restroom

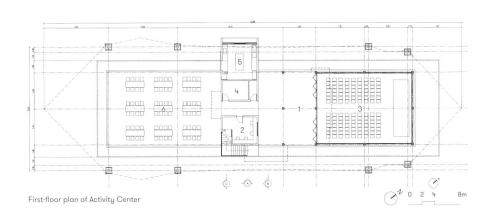

First-floor plan of Activity Center

0 2 4   8m

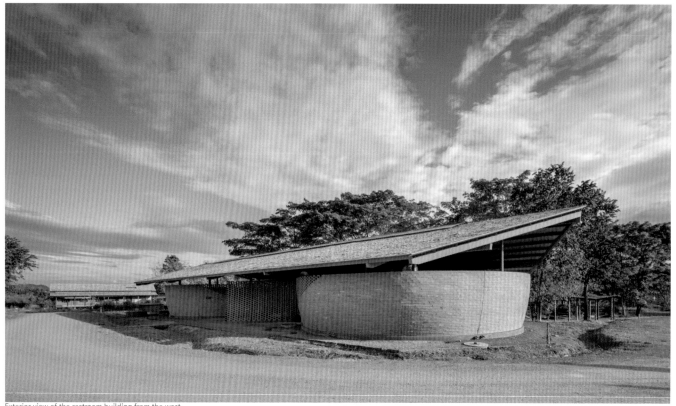
Exterior view of the restroom building from the west

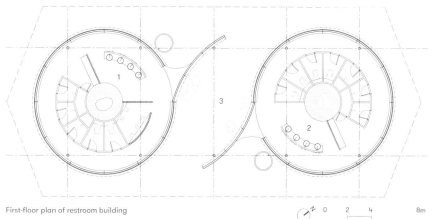
First-floor plan of restroom building

1.   Men's restroom
2.   Women's restroom
3.   Waiting area

N   0   2   4   8m

Interior of the women's restroom

Elevations of Activity Center

Sections of Activity Center

0 2 4   8m

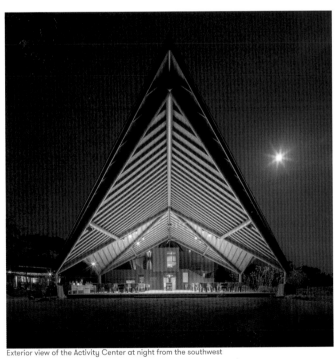

Exterior view of the Activity Center at night from the southwest

Exterior view of the restroom building at night

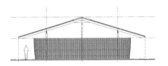

Elevations of restroom building

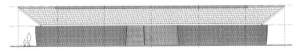

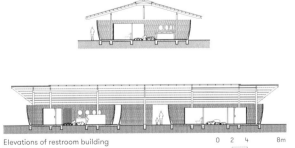

Elevations of restroom building

0 2 4   8m

Duriflex Warehouse

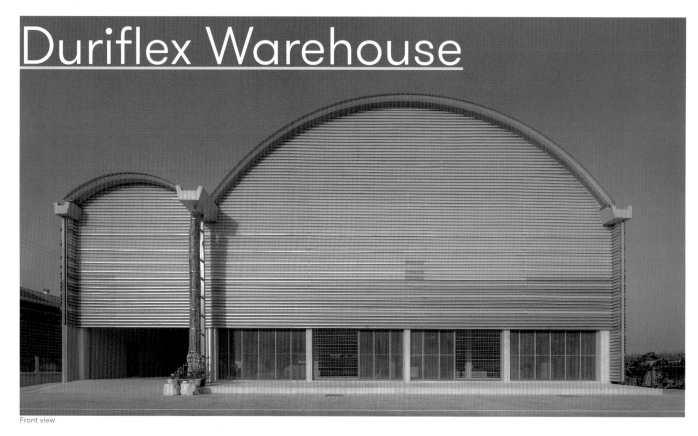

Front view

Architect firm: all[zone]
Principal architect: Rachaporn Choochuey
Design team: Rachaporn Choochuey,
Ruchanan Patarapanich, Aniroot Unjai
Location: Samut Sakhon Province, Thailand
Area: 2,412 square meters
Completion date: August 2019
Photography: Soopakorn Srisakul

In a prominent industrial neighborhood on the fringe of Bangkok, Thailand, stands the headquarter of Duriflex. For decades, its made-to-order production has led the local furniture market. The organization's growing dead stock called for an expansion that would create a new display/storage space, where customers could also walk-in.

Executed mainly in utilitarian aspects, like most industrial buildings, the new Duriflex warehouse is roofed with two lightweight structural vaults made of folded metal sheets, which results in the minimum use of material for a long-span coverage.

The big vault covers the main storage spaces on both levels. The small vault serves as the main entrance and loading area, leading customers to the upper level where the products are displayed. The building assimilates with its surrounding through the application of generic materials widely used on local industrial architecture. A breathing skin of translucent and opaque louvers filters the strong tropical light—while still allowing enough natural light

in—as it facilitates total natural ventilation in the interior. This enables zero energy consumption in the daytime.

Amid the company's supply stock, is a wooden log believed to be the home of a local spirit, looked upon as a blessed protector that is revered by the factory workers. To respect the workers' belief and

honor their reverence for this log, it is given its own superrational placement instead of being unceremoniously stored away among the furniture stock.

This sacred log has been erected on the front façade and consecrated as the spiritual pillar of the building to support, protect, and bring good fortune to the company.

South view

Main entrance

Loading area leading to the upper floor

A breathing skin of translucent and opaque louvers filters strong tropical light

89

Display of products on the upper floor under a large vault

Long-spanned coverage made from folded metal sheets

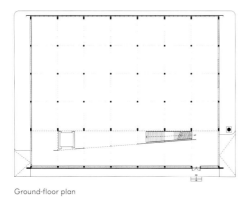

Ground-floor plan

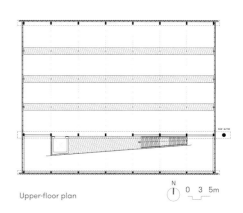

Upper-floor plan

N   0 3 5m

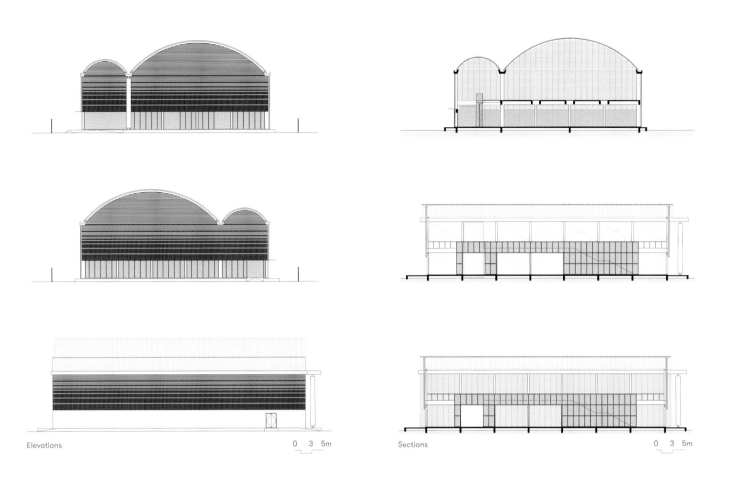

Elevations   0 3 5m   Sections   0 3 5m

View from the upper level

Radial House

The south elevation viewed from across the lake

Architect firm: Stu/D/O Architects
Principal architect: Apichart Srirojanapinyo
Design team: Apichart Srirojanapinyo,
Chanasit Cholasuek, Supachart Boontang,
Patompong Songpracha
Location: Nakhon Ratchasima, Thailand
Area: 1,100 square meters
Completion date: July 2020
Photography: DOF Sky|Ground

Surrounded by the mountains and greenery of Khao Yai National Park in Nakhon Ratchasima, Thailand, this family vacation home along the water's edge is a multi-generational residence for the owner's family to enjoy time away from the city. Tailored with a layout that allows members of each generation to gather and socialize among themselves, within their own group space, this project provides an ideal venue for both rest and recreation within Khao Yai's compelling natural scenery.

Located right on the bend of a large body of water, the building is integrated into the nature surrounding it, highlighting a sloping mass that blends into the site, which opens up to panoramic views of the lake in front and the mountains beyond. The project's main design focus is centered on the living areas of the multigeneration spaces, to successfully enable its function as a vacation home. Thus, the program is arranged in two distinct volumes: a calm and composed family area for the parents on the ground level, and an elevated party space for the children set further along the curve. These two living quarters are arranged along the water's edge, separated by a large tree court and in altering levels, but still connected with each other by the

sloping vertical circulation that becomes the main formal element of the architecture.

The slope connects the two living/leisure areas together. Its dynamic form encourages interaction and connection between the two spaces and its users. A tertiary space, formed by the gentle slope of the concrete floor, highlights the radial quality of the site, which completely opens up to a dazzling scenery framed by the water and mountains beyond. As the sloping element in the architecture connects the two leisure areas, its elevation also permits a separation between the two volumes and the users within them. As a family that frequently enjoys hosting and entertaining guests, the distinct spaces allow each generation to host gatherings and activities for their respective group of guests.

The spatial organization sets a main private quarter with three bedrooms that sits atop the family living area on the east, while another two-bedroom guest quarter—in cross with the slope—is interlocked under the children's party/leisure area on the west. The two areas are independent of each other, but connected by the sloping roof, which creates coherence between the two volumes.

Even though high ceilings have been designed in this two-story home, the intent was to keep as much of the volume within the horizontal plane as possible, to blend the architecture with the landscape, leaving the mountain scenery and surrounding nature to take centerstage and create an engulfing effect. The spatial organization and radial-like form of the house help achieve this; arranging the program along the soft slope induces, and enhances, the planar quality.

The spacious terrace below the east wing's sleeping quarter is a semi-outdoor

living space that opens up to the internal courtyard; it flows seamlessly into the open void of the sloping mass, creating natural ventilation, while encouraging inhabitants to be outdoors and among nature. The languid contour of the slope conveys a relaxing atmosphere, as intended, and teams with a carefully selected material palette enhance this ambiance. Raw concrete is employed in its materiality to achieve the required formwork of the slope; wood adds warmth to the interior and exterior of the home; and Nero Marquina marble highlights certain areas, to impart a sense of solidity to the overall scheme. This natural palette plays off the surrounding natural landscape while adding materiality to the house.

The main bedroom is located on the second floor, on top of the living area

Aerial view highlighting the relationship between the curved living area and the lake

From the drop-off area looking east

Campfire area next to the lake

Looking toward the house from the drop-off and parking area

Semi-outdoor courtyard under the curved roof

Semi-outdoor breakfast and party area

Looking toward the side courtyard from the semi-outdoor breakfast and party area

Family room on the upper floor

Main bedroom

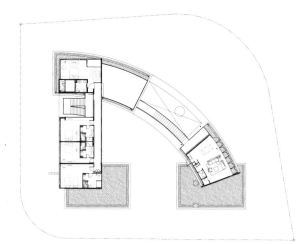

Second-floor plan

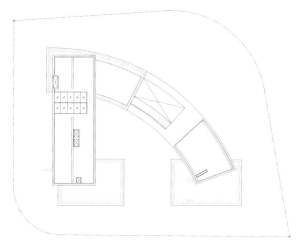

Rooftop floor plan

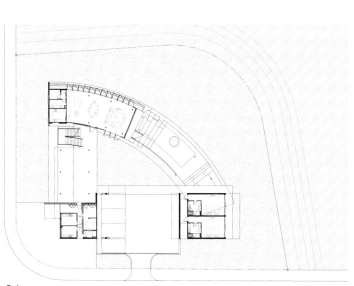

First-floor plan

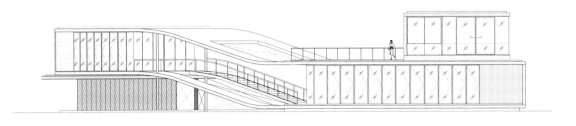

Elevations

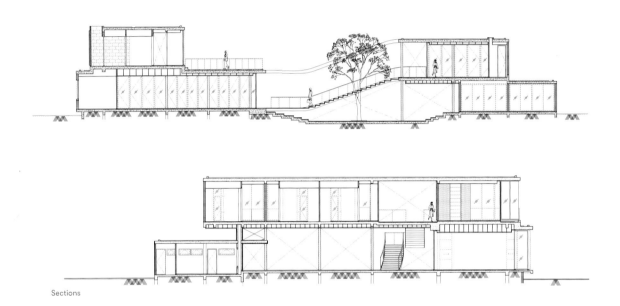

Sections

Guest bedroom quarter

97

Livist Resort Petchabun

Overall view of resort

Architect firm: Patchara + Ornnicha
Architecture (POAR)
Principal architect: Patchara Wongboonsin,
Ornnicha Duriyaprapan
Design team: Patchara Wongboonsin,
Prakai Voranisarakul, Ornnicha Duriyaprapan,
Pongsakon Ponpaiboon, Sakrawut Suma,
Chanont Kaeklang, Panchika Trisukosol
Location: Petchabun, Thailand
Area: 8,000 square meters
Completion date: December 2020
Photography: Patchara Wongboonsin,
Kukkong Thirathomrongkiat,
Papon Kasettratat

The open-air pool is enfolded by a collection of fourteen inverted pyramid structures that also double as supports for cultivating perennial plants. A length that spans 3.5 meters allows the sheltered space to breathe and form a conjoined pocket space that that tempts guests with an inviting swimming experience. The area feels simultaneously ensconced, yet open and airy without compromising privacy, encouraging an extended use of the swimming pool.

The overgrown Callistemon viminalis trees planted in cast-in-place exposed concrete structures alter the pool scenery with

the seasons and lend a tropical ambiance to the pool area.

The vessel design concept of the pool composes a two-layered circle. The outer layer is a sunbathing space that incorporates the children's pool, which gradually slopes into the center of the inner circle. This design allows multiple entrance points and displays the pool depth through silhouettes of the dark, locally sourced marble tiles on the base of the pool. At night, reflections on the rippling water surface transform submerged planters into light sculptures, creating an almost ethereal aquatic land.

Livist Resort is a city hotel located in the center of Petchabun, Thailand, and is situated forty minutes away from natural attractions like the dreamlike Khao Kho District set in a sea of clouds. The hotel, surrounded by small local dwellings, features an all-day swimming pool, which makes it especially popular among leisure travelers who are on the look-out for extended activities. Located in the garden situated in the west wing of the hotel, the swimming pool awards guests a glorious view of Khao Kho's sunset scenery.

Pool landscape

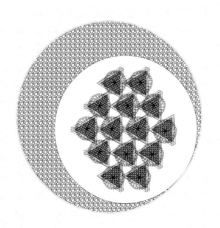

Livist Resort's swimming pool floor plan

Promenade between houses

Entrance view

The inverted pyramid structures that "emerge" from the water double as supports to grow a plant canopy

View of pool from balcony of guestroom

View of pool at night

View of the resort's restaurant at night

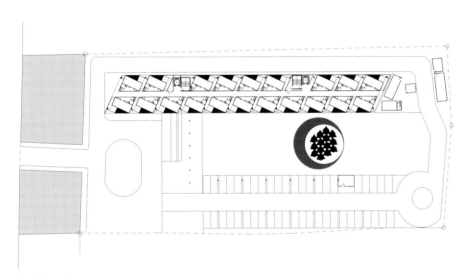

Overall floor plan

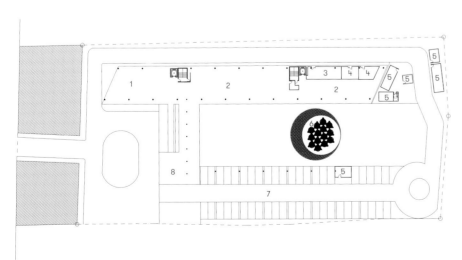

Ground-floor plan

1. Lobby
2. Restaurant
3. Kitchen
4. Building system
5. Service
6. Swimming pool
7. Parking
8. Drop-off

Interior of guestroom

The rooftop swimming pool treats guests to great sunset sceneries

Reflections in the pool give the impression of a seemingly alternate dimension

At night, the pool takes on an almost ethereal appearance with lighted planters and iridescent reflections that dazzle the water surface

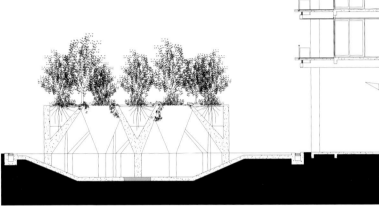

Section—swimming pool building

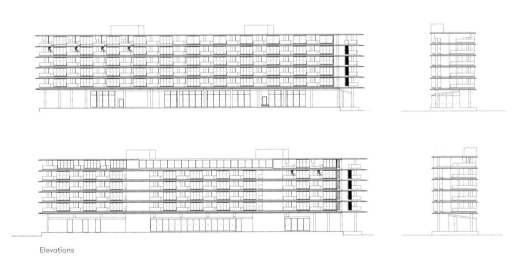

Elevations

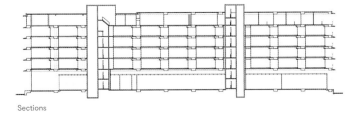

Sections

Pusayapuri Hotel

Pusayapuri commemorates the forgotten history of U-Thong city, making the lost appear again, but in a form that doesn't have to be complete; it is an acceptance of the reality of what has been lost, while maintaining the condition of what remains to create a new chapter of history in another form

Architect firm: EKAR Architects
Principal architect: Ekaphap Duangkaew
Design team: Ekaphap Duangkaew,
Tirayon Khunpukdee, Sirisak Thammasiri
Location: Authong, Suphan Buri, Thailand
Area: 3,138 square meters
Completion date: December 2022
Photography: Rungkit Charoenwat

This six-level complex of serviced apartments has been developed to cater to Suphan Buri, Thailand, as a new cultural tourism locale in Thailand. A clever design increases the public space in the complex as one ascends the building. Each modular wall is connected by recessing the corner, which allows more green space on each ascending floor than the one before. Inspired by the heavy base of Buddhist stupas, the 45-centimeter-thick wall filters heat and dissipates it where direct sunlight hits the façade.

Given the love he has for his hometown, building owner Werawat Luangwechakarn intends for the architecture of Pusayapuri Hotel to reawaken the glorious town in which it resides. He also hopes it will present Authong, Suphan Buri, as a historically significant town in Thailand.

The project's initial requirements were different from other buildings of the same nature. The owner wanted the building to first convey the character of Authong, placing its role as a functional apartment second. The building's location by the road that leads to the downtown area provided an advantage, as it naturally presents Pusayapuri as the gateway to Authong.

Thai Traits are the Building's Architectural Characteristics

The architecture of Pusayapuri Hotel, in a sense, serves as a memorial of Authong as it reflects an experimentation with the physical appearances of the "Thai image," be they a gabled structure or the superimposition of layers that reflect a sense of Thai identity and aesthetics. Thai traits are derived from a high level of intricateness, which is an integral part of the Thai identity that is weaved into every aspect of the iterations of Thai architecture. In this project, such intricateness combines with inspiration gathered from historical remains found in Authong—the ruins of the base of an ancient stupa—to realize the design of the building through the simplified details of the recessed corners commonly found in the construction of Buddhist stupas in the area. The building's functionality was then created through a systematic projection and recess of the façade.

The location of the building turns it to face west; parts of the façade are projected 70 centimeters, serving as eaves for the rooms. This projected space is designed into a bay window in standard rooms without an outdoor area, with a floor-to-ceiling glass opening, and as a terrace for rooms with an exterior railing. Each piece of the modular façade measures 3 × 2.5 meters; installation was carried out on a coated galvanized steel structure jointed to the structural wall.

Another highlighted element is the material used with the façade. Glass-fiber reinforced-concrete (GFRC) was selected as the façade material instead of red bricks—even though the bricks would lend a rustic

authenticity with their materiality—to navigate issues like weight limitation, construction techniques, structural safety, and considerations of seismic resilience. The strength, light weight, and surface properties of GFRC made it ideal for the project, and also since it was available in a color that matched the design requirements, all that was left to do was consider the coating. Contemporary iterations of Thai characteristics were defined through the use of a new material. With the help of technology, the past and present clash beautifully, like the musical notes of a symphonic composition.

In this project, architecture serves its primary role to generate new questions and bring a greater dynamic to the city it is located in. It triggers people's interest in their own cultural, historical, and familial background and roots; the connection between the past and present is made more visible through the presence of the built structure. The flexibility extended to amend the original design idea—with the understanding and acceptance of the owner—provides the building the possibility to extend its benefits to many other dimensions. The rewards do not only go back to the success of the business of the serviced apartments, but also to the people of Authong, as the history of this once glorious port city of the nation is reintroduced to gain a much wider recognition.

Sky garden atrium—a garden area on a wide terrace that is open and airy; the design of the pagoda inspires planters that also double as seats

Swimming pool entrance 1: a walkway connects the building and the garden through an opening in the façade

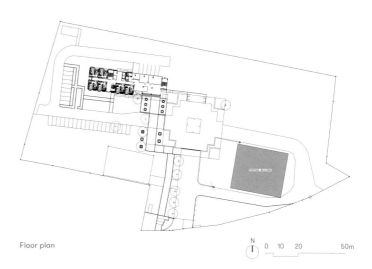
Floor plan

N   0   10   20   50m

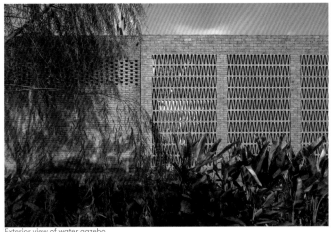
Exterior view of water gazebo

Interior view of water gazebo

Sky garden atrium—a garden area on a wide terrace that is open and airy; the design of the pagoda inspires planters that also double as seats

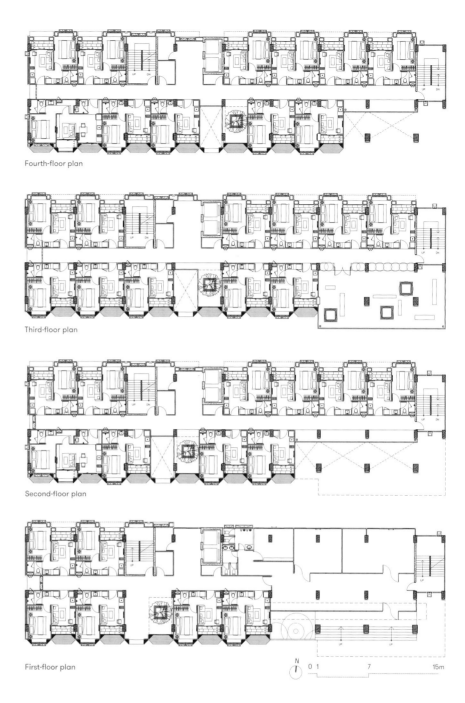

Fourth-floor plan

Third-floor plan

Second-floor plan

First-floor plan

N
0 1   7   15m

Swimming pool entrance 2: view from within looking out onto the walkway connecting to the pool

Waiting area

Stacking of the six stories of the atrium

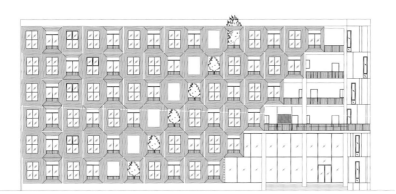 

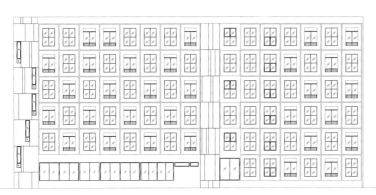 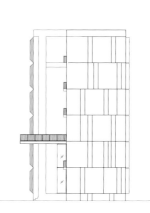

Elevations

 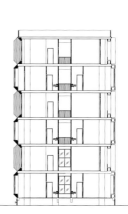

TONGJI
ARCHITECTURAL DESIGN
(GROUP) CO., LTD.

Exterior of the TJAD office building

ABOUT TJAD

Tongji Architectural Design (Group) Co., Ltd. (TJAD), formerly known as the Architectural Design and Research Institute of Tongji University, was founded in 1958 and has now developed into a well-known large-scale design and consulting group.

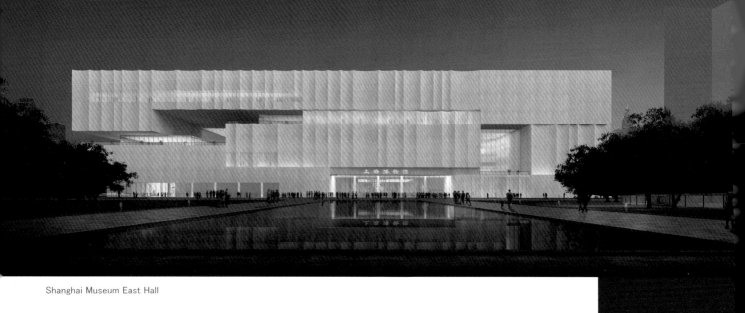

Shanghai Museum East Hall

With almost seventy years of history behind it, and with the profound cultural foundation of Tongji University, TJAD has accumulated a rich experience in both engineering design and technical consultancy, progressing notably over the last sixty-five years. TJAD is a design institution with one of the most extensive design qualifications in China, with a business scope that includes consulting, engineering design, project management, geotechnical engineering, and geological exploration in the fields of building engineering, road engineering, municipal engineering, landscape engineering, environmental pollution prevention, and conservation of historical and cultural relics, among others. The organization has embarked on thousands of projects in China, Africa, and South America that include, among many, Shanghai Tower, Fangfei Garden of the Diaoyutai State Guest House, Table Tennis Gymnasium of the 2008 Olympic Games, African Union Conference Center, New Jinggangshan Revolution Museum, Shanghai Xintiandi, Theme Pavilion of the 2010 Shanghai Expo, Shanghai International Tourist Resort, Shanghai Natural History Museum, Shanghai Symphony Orchestra Concert Hall, China Corporate United Pavilion of Expo 2015 Milan, Havana Hotel of Cuba, Saikang Di Stadium of the Republic of Ghana, the National Arts Center of the Republic of Trinidad and Tobago, Sutong Yangtze River Highway Bridge, and Shanghai A5 (Jiading-Jinshan) Expressway Project.

Shanghai Tower
(Cooperative Design,
in partnership with
Gensler, Cosentini, and
Thornton Tomasetti)

Museum of Art Pudong
(Cooperative Design,
in partnership with
Ateliers Jean Nouvel)

Xi'an International Convention and Exhibition Center (Cooperative Design, in partnership with gmp and WES)

TJAD employs more than five thousand outstanding architectural design and engineering personnel to provide top engineering consulting services for our clients, and we have been working hard to promote urban development, so that we may build a better life for citizens through our many professional practices.

We firmly believe that it is the trust that our clients have in us that gives TJAD opportunities to grow. As part of the society and industry, we strive to continue to channel unremitting efforts toward industry development and social progress, just like we have been doing the past sixty-five years.

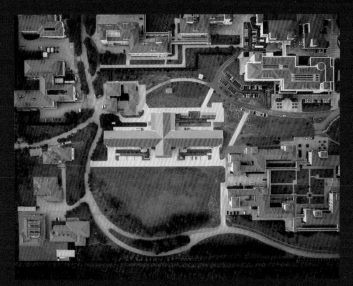

Contingency and Temporary Medical Building of Shanghai Public Health Clinical Center

Shangyin Opera House (Cooperative Design, in partnership with Christian de Portzamparc, Xu-Acoustique, and Theater Projects Consultants)

Green Hill, Shanghai

TONGJI ARCHITECTURAL DESIGN (GROUP) CO., LTD., (TJAD)

VISION

Become a respected design and engineering consultancy with global influence

MISSION

Enable people to live and work in a better place with our creative labor

CORE VALUES

Focus on customers and grow together with employees

SPIRIT

Work together and pursue excellence

Address: No.1230 Siping Road, Shanghai, China, 200092

Telephone: 0086-21-65987788

Email: 5wjia@tjad.cn

Web: www.tjad.cn